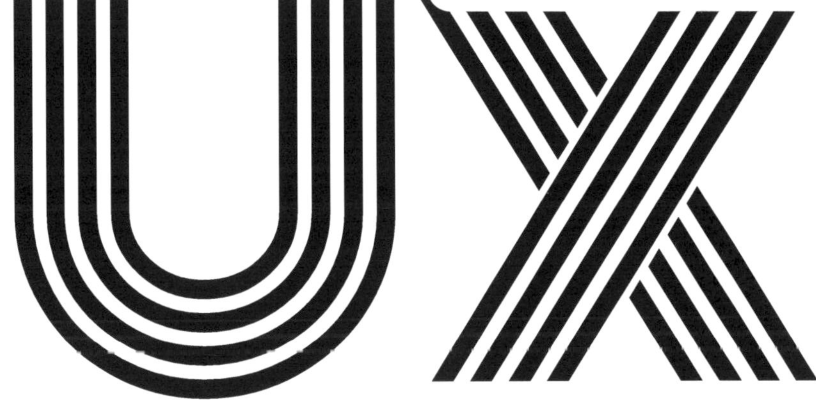

UX METHODS

A QUICK GUIDE TO USER EXPERIENCE RESEARCH METHODS

JAMES PANNAFINO AND PATRICK MCNEIL

Reviews

"James Pannafino and Patrick McNeil have managed to break down a huge range of very complex user research and usability testing methods into simple, easy to digest explanations with real life application examples. *UX Methods* is an exceptional resource and should be required reading for those who are new to the industry. It's also an excellent source of inspiration for seasoned UX veterans, especially when tackling complex problems."
– Jennifer Aldrich, UX & Content Strategist at InVisionApp

"The book provides a thorough list of methods for collecting and validating UX requirements. It provides a great intro for beginners, and it provides a great cheat sheet for seasoned veterans. These methods are an integral part of my design process, and I use them on a daily basis. The provided examples really bring the methods to life."
– Kent Eisenhuth, UX Designer at Google

"*UX Methods* is an invaluable tool kit for building great stuff. It makes me wish I had every page printed out on the wall next to me at all times for review. Even the most experienced practitioner needs to be reminded how to build with user focused, easy to understand collaboration, which this publication does brilliantly."
– Alexander Reyna, Director, Experience Design, MLB Advanced Media

"*UX Methods* covers a broad range of methods in a way that is both thorough and concise. A must-have resource for any professional or student in a UX design field. I recommend all UX teams have a copy for reference."
– Victor Yocco, PhD, UX Research Director at EY Intuitive

Please Read First

All information provided in this book is either based on professional referenced research, personal experience, common knowledge or professional feedback. The authors have worked hard to present correct and current information in this book. They cannot assure that all the information will fit every situation or is completely in line with each discipline's perspective.

Copyright © 2017 by James Pannafino and Patrick McNeil
ISBN: 978-0-692-97271-7
Library of Congress Control Number: 2017916028

www.uxmethodsbook.com
Published by CDUXP LLC

Book and Cover Design: James Pannafino

About the Authors

James Pannafino

James Pannafino is an Associate Professor at Millersville University in Pennsylvania. He teaches web, interaction, experience and motion design courses for the (BDes) Bachelor of Design degree. His research interests include interactive design fundamentals, interdisciplinary design, visual storytelling and digital narrative forms. James wrote and published *Interdisciplinary Interaction Design: A Visual Guide to Basic Theories, Models and Ideas for Thinking and Designing for Interactive Web Design and Digital Device Experiences*.

www.jamespannafino.com
www.interdisciplinaryinteractiondesign.com

Patrick McNeil

Patrick McNeil is a UX Architect and passionate advocate of users everywhere. He holds a master's degree in Human-Computer Interaction and has a long history in both technology and design. Patrick is the creator of Design Meltdown, and the author of *The Web Designer's Idea Book* series and *The Mobile Web Designer's Idea Book*.

www.pmcncil.com
www.thewebdesignersideabook.com

Table of Contents

1   GETTING STARTED

4   2X2 Matrix

6   A/B Testing

8   Analytic Insights

10   AS-IS and TO-BE Analysis

12   Backcasting Method

14   Bodystorming

16   Business Origami

18   Card Sorting

20   Claims Analysis

22   Cognitive Walkthrough

24   Competitivc Analysis

26   Concept Model Process

28   Contextual Inquiry

30   Desirability Studies

32   Elito Method

34   Emoticon Score Method

36   Empathy Interview

38   Empathy Map

40   Field Studies

42   First Click Test

44   Five Second Test

46   Five Whys Analysis

48   Freelisting

50   Future Workshop

52   Guerrilla Usability Testing

54 Heuristic Evaluation

56 Hot Air Balloon

58 I Like, I Wish, What If

60 Icon Usability Test

62 Informal Usability Testing

64 Interviewing Users

66 Journey Map

68 Keyboard Level Modeling

70 Photojournal

72 Pluralistic Walkthrough

74 Rapid User Profile

76 Real Time Conversational Feedback

78 RITE Method

80 Semantic Differential Analysis

82 Sentence Completion

84 Single Ease Question (SEQ)

86 Static Evaluation and Markup

88 Storyboarding for UX

90 Surveys

92 System Usability Scale

94 Teachback

96 Trade-Off Sliders

98 UX Curve

100 Value Proposition Generation

102 Wizard of Oz Studies

104 REFERENCES

107 IMAGE CREDITS

X

Getting Started

This book is designed to provide a wide range of research methods with concise instructions that enable you to jump in and try the method out. Each method has a visual example that seeks to provide greater understanding on how that method might be used.

The intent of this book is not to define an overall process, but there are some considerations before jumping in and using a method. For example, knowing what questions you seek answers to is a great first step. Outlined here are a few things to help frame the methods that are provided.

Writing a Research Question

In order to conduct effective research you must first know what you seek to learn. What are the questions you want answered? What is it you don't know about your users? This is the foundation for building a research question. A research question is simply an expression of what you seek to learn.

Examples include:
"Which version of my design will users understand best?"
"What are the most prominent usability problems with my design?"
"How can I prioritize features to add to my product?'

Knowing what you need to learn is a simple step that makes your selection of a research method much more strategic and meaningful. Simply think about what you need or want to learn about your product; then write a question that reflects this.

A great extra step is to consider what you will do with the answers to the questions. Sometimes a research question sounds important, but the results of the work won't change your course of action. This extra step will help you avoid wasted time on research.

Selecting a Research Method

Once you have your research questions you are ready to select a research method. Each method is able to provide answers to certain types of questions. Most of the methods in this book are very open ended and can be modified to provide different types of answers. In fact, the more you dig in and creatively seek answers, the more you will find yourself creating your own research methods.

Carefully consider what you seek to learn and if a given method will help you discover that information. Sometimes this is an easy decision, but in other cases it is much harder to figure out how to find answers.

At the bottom of the first page for each method are some useful elements that will aid you in your selection process. First, you will find a When to Use section. This features generalized statements about when this particular method might apply. Sometimes this is a certain time in the design process. In other cases it is more the type of information you need to gather.

You will also find at the bottom of each page basic attributes of the method. This includes a rough estimate of how difficult or easy the method is, how long it might take and how many participants (or users) might be needed. Please keep in mind that these are general numbers and are often just a starting point. In some cases the number of participants can vary greatly depending on how the method is to be used.

Documenting Results

Sharing the results of your research is almost as important as the research itself. You can easily scale the amount of documentation to fit the environment you work in. If you're in a small start-up that just needs to make fast decisions, you might not document at all. If you're in a corporate setting where you need a modest trail of what has transpired, then do so. Typically it is best to capture the **when, what, how and why.**

In all cases, the executive summary will be your best friend. Regardless of how long your results document is you should always make one of the very first pages an executive summary. This single page should summarize what you researched, the key results and the most significant action items. This quick summary will not only help ensure people read it, but also will remind you of what you found later down the road.

2X2 Matrix

A 2x2 matrix is a way to compare a product or experiences by visually mapping them based on contrasting attributes within a 2 by 2 grid.

Draw out two axes, one vertical and one horizontal crossing each to form a 2 by 2 grid. On one line at both ends, put two values that are opposite of each other, such as "high cost" and "low cost." Then do the same with the other line using different attributes, such as "many features" vs "single feature." Then begin to position items on the 2 by 2 grid that you would like to compare. This can be done on whiteboard at first for quick adjustments and a more refined digital version later for reports and archiving purposes.

Once the items are mapped out you can observe many things. For example, large empty spaces on the matrix might represent opportunities in the marketplace. These same holes might even represent segments of the market that have no demand and should be avoided. Careful consideration should be given to the matrix as you interpret it and use it as a tool.

A common approach is to map the same items on multiple 2x2 Matrixes, each with different attributes on the two axis. This gives you multiple ways to view the same items in order to gain a better understanding of how the items relate to each other.

When to use: To better determine your relationship to competitors.

Difficulty: Average   **Time:** 4 Hours   **Participants:** 2+

2x2 Matrix Example

In this example, a new personal health product is going to be considered. The company wants to assess the direct competition and see if there is a niche to fill. The 2x2 matrix method allows for the team to see an overview of each product's values and a broad comparison with other products that already exist.

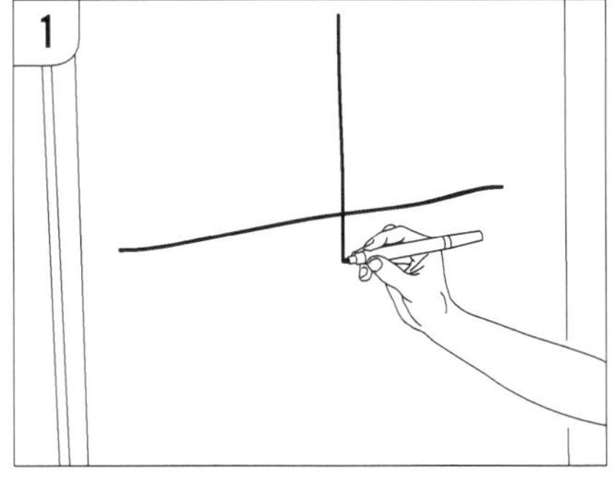

Establish Matrix: On a whiteboard, draw the 2x2 matrix grid by creating crossing horizontal and vertical lines.

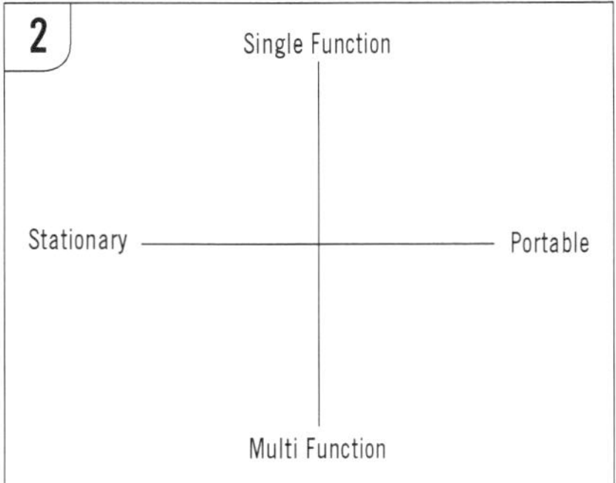

Map Values: At each end of the matrix lines add comparative values such as "portable" vs. "stationary" and "multi function" vs. "single function" that best frame the new digital product.

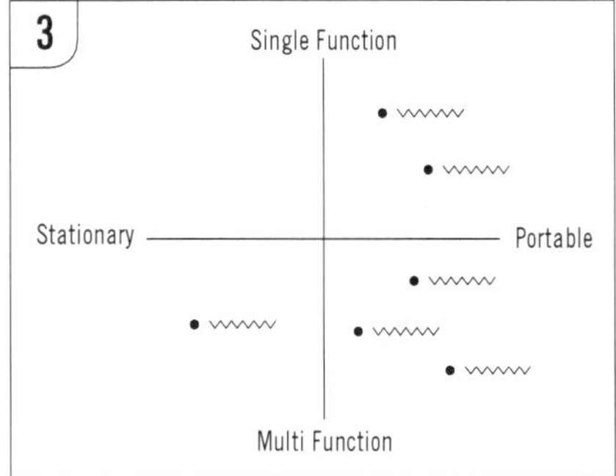

Position Items: Place existing competitors into the matrix based on the comparative values.

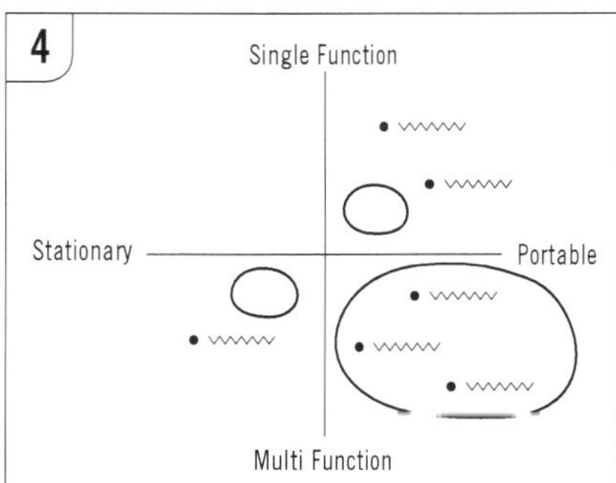

Review Results: The team can review the completed matrix to see where there is overlap and new opportunities.

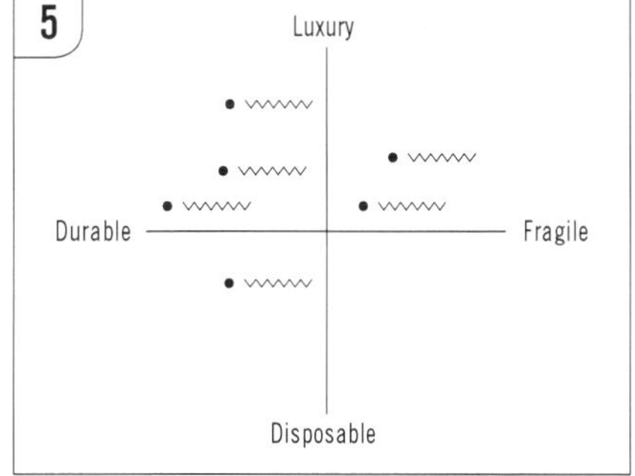

Repeat with Different Values: The process can be repeated for the same product using different values such as "durable" vs. "fragile" and "luxury" vs. "disposable."

A/B Testing

A/B testing is a method used to compare two designs against each other to see which one produces the best results.

First, you must have two versions of the design. The difference between the two designs could be almost anything from a small design detail to a radically new layout. A common approach is to use the current design as one option and create a new variation as the alternate. These will be your A and B versions.

Next, determine what you will be measuring and how you will determine which design is better. This metric should be easily measured so you can determine the preferred design approach. For example you could select user preference or click through rate as a metric.

Finally, put the design in front of at least 10 users and measure the results. From this you should discover if the new version improves the desired outcome (click throughs, user understanding, etc.).

There are many tools available to easily run A/B tests and collect the results. Using an online tool is probably the easiest and fastest way to get started. Oftentimes A/B tests are performed on live products using real users in order to optimize a site's performance.

When to use: When you want to understand the impact of design changes.

Difficulty: Average   **Time:** 1 Hour   **Participants:** 10+

A/B Testing Example

In this example the designer has an idea for how to improve a page but is unsure if users will like the change. An A/B test will help discover the user's preference.

Identify the Focus: The designer wants to see if changes to the design will help users understand the product better.

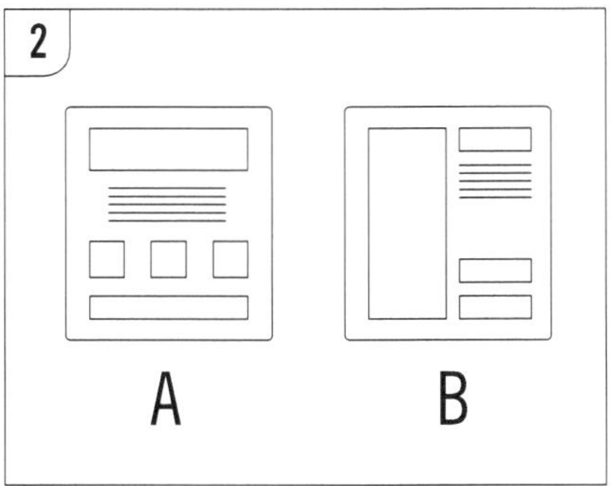

Create the Test: The designer creates a new version of the screen to compare to the original.

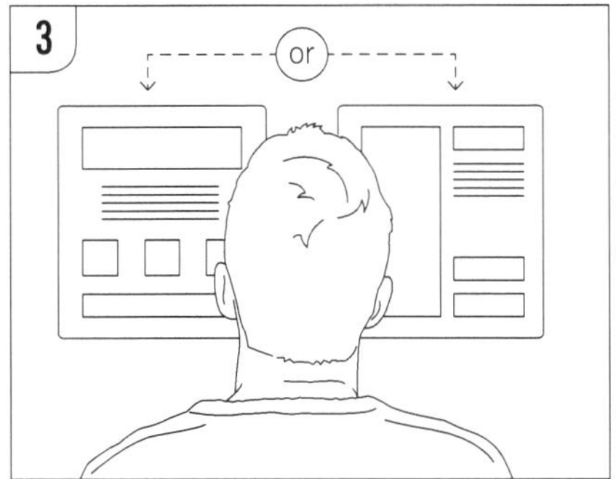

Test the Design: Each participant is shown both designs and is asked which version they prefer. The test is repeated with 10 different participants.

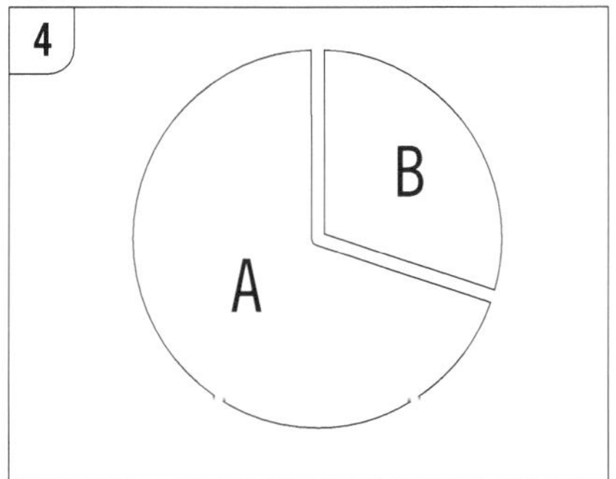

Analyze the Results: Compare the results to identify which design users tend to prefer. The degree to which users prefer one to the other can also be helpful.

Implement the Results: The designer knows which version of the design to use.

Analytic Insights

Analytics are used to measure actual utilization of a product, how many users there are and what activities they do within the digital product.

Getting analytics set up on your product is fairly simple. Select your analytics tool and attach it to your product. This typically involves adding a small amount of code to your product to enable the analytics tool to track and store data about your users.

Once installed, the analytics tool will track the activity of users within your product. This will give you insight into the pages and functionality that users access most. It can also be configured to track more advanced things like conversion rates - or the number of visitors that take a desired action like making a purchase.

Keep in mind that analytics will only show you how frequently users are accessing and using various features within your website or application. Analytics will not show you if they were satisfied with the experience or if they wanted to do something your product doesn't do.

Analytics are useful when calculating the ROI of feature changes. Being able to measure exactly how often something happens enables you to more accurately calculate its value.

When to use: Any time real user metrics are benefitial.

Difficulty: Average   **Time:** 4 Hours   **Participants:** 10+

Analytics Insights Example

In this example there are numerous requests to add features to a music app. Without data it is hard to know which features will be of the most value. Analytics will help by tracking utilization and provide data on how frequently these parts of the app are used.

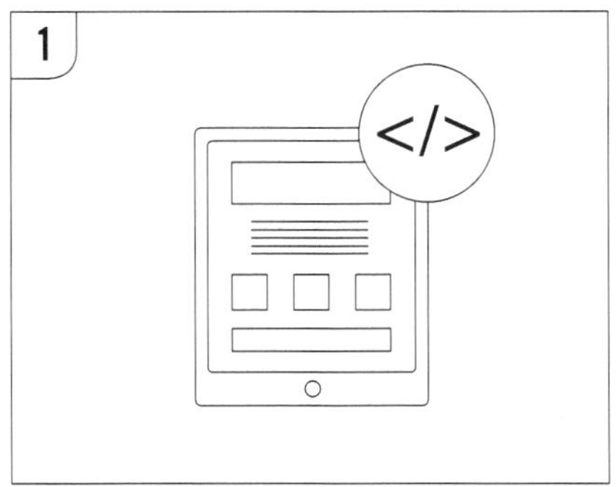

Set Up Tracking Tool: Add the analytics tool to the app in order to start tracking usage of specific sections.

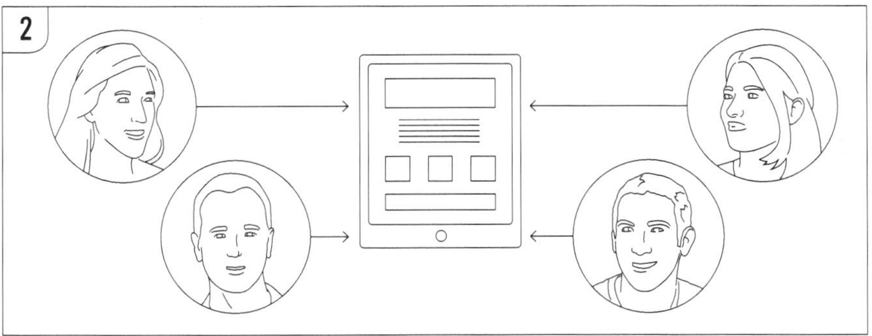

Collect Data: User activity is collected for several weeks to provide sufficient data.

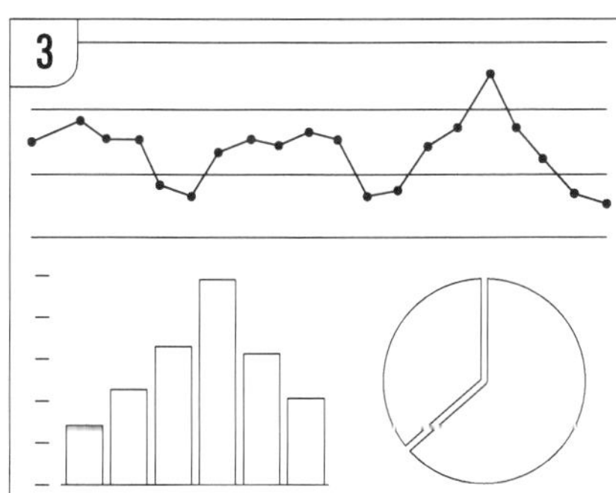

Report: The analytics package creates a report showing how frequently each tracked section is used.

Make a Decision: With the data collected the team is able to identify which section is most used and can focus on feature requests in that area.

AS-IS and TO-BE Analysis

AS-IS and TO-BE is a visual comparison method where the current state (as-is) of the product or system is shown next to the future (to-be) state.

First, establish the user goals and targeted user persona (page 74). Visually map out the current state of the product. Most often this is done in the form of a flow chart. Create notations on the visual map pointing out adjustment areas, or components you intend to modify. Next, create a new visual map that shows the future state and possible solutions. Finally, place both current and future visual map states next to each other and discuss the effects and outcomes.

This simple before and after analysis can be extremely helpful to teams as they consider potential changes to a system. This visual artifact not only clarifies things for a team but also helps them to discover unintended consequences to potential changes.

Another benefit of this method is that, in some cases, it can be difficult for non-users of a system to understand the significance of even small changes to the workflow. By visualizing them side-by-side these important nuances can be more fully understood.

When to use: When a feature in a product or system needs improvement and a new version is being considered.

Difficulty: Average   **Time:** 1 Hour   **Participants:** 0

AS-IS and TO-BE Analysis Example

In this example a new prescription delivery system is being considered. We want to see if the new system is more effective for the user compared to the old one. This comparison method is a direct way to see if the new system is an improvement over the current system.

Determine Direction: First, review the personas to make sure the proper users are being addressed.

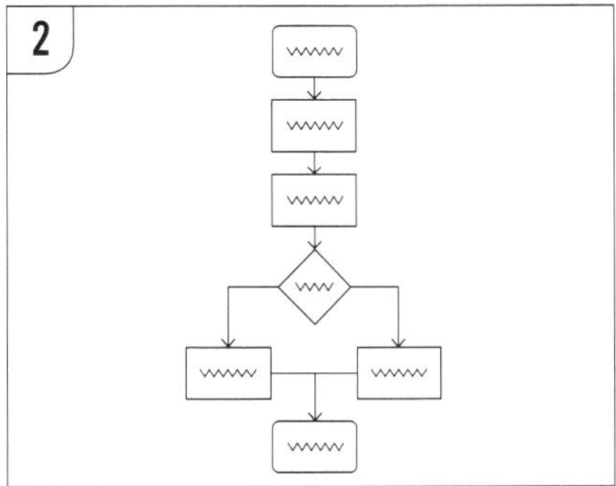

Map Out Current AS-IS State: Using a visual mapping language, show the current state to better understand the situation.

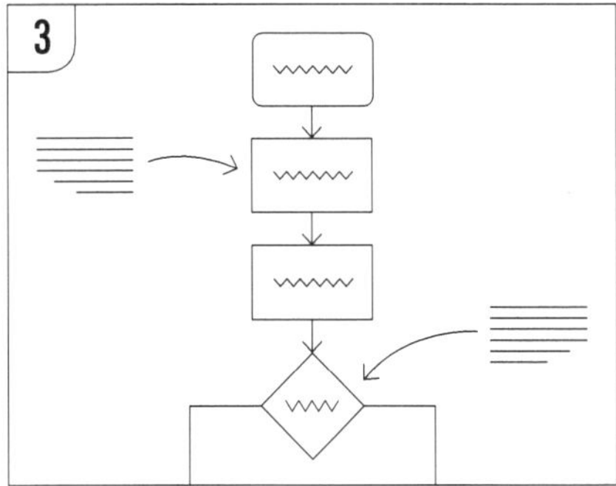

Notate Adjustment Points: Mark where there might be issues in the current process that can be addressed in the new version.

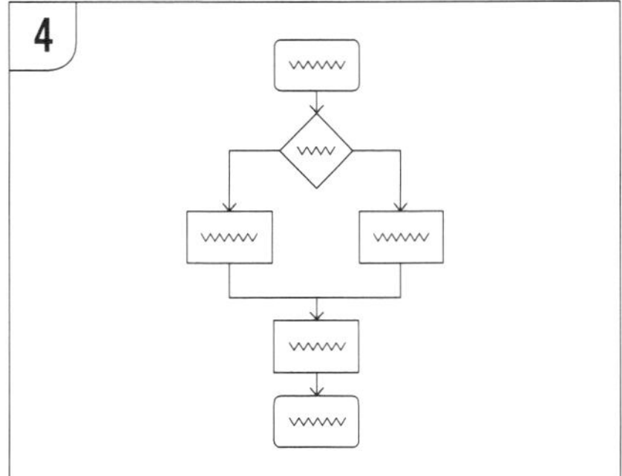

Map Out Future TO-BE Path: Using the persona and reference notes from the current process, map out an alternative version that improves the user's experience.

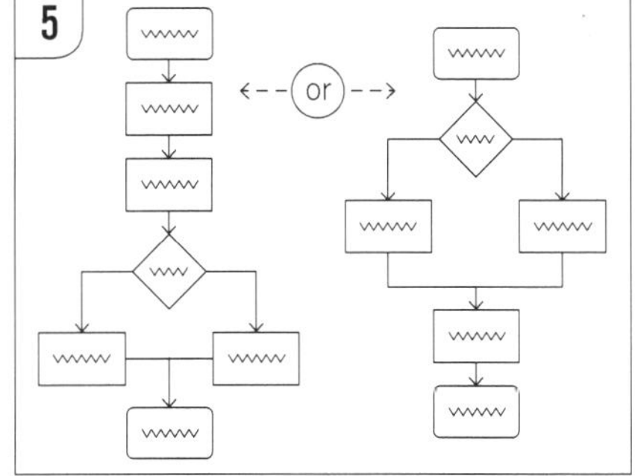

Analyze Directions: Place both processes next to each other (AS-IS left / TO-BE right) and discuss which one affords the best result for the user.

Method Reference: *Agile Experience Design: A Digital Designer's Guide to Agile, Lean, and Continuous,* November 28, 2011 by Lindsay Ratcliffe and Marc McNeill.

Backcasting Method

Use initial research to create a future vision for your project, then work backwards to create a plan to get to the desired destination.

This method begins by reviewing the existing research for your project. This might include usability tests (pages 52, 62 and 78), user interviews (page 64), analytics (page 8) or any other data you have collected.

Based on these user insights the team should form different ideas for what the project might look like in the future. These should be high level ideas that represent large steps for the product. From these options the team should select a single vision to work towards.

Once the vision is established, you can lay out a rough plan with all the steps and actions to get to that future desired destination. This should include key milestones marking the way to the end goal. As the product is being built, it can be tempting to get lost in the details and find yourself distracted by other short term goals. Having a long term vision to focus on can help keep things moving along and the team focused on the big goal.

When to use: When you know what you want, but need to create a plan to get there.

Difficulty: Very Hard   **Time:** 4 Hours   **Participants:** 10+

Backcasting Method Example

In this example a team is planning a new piece of software to track all of the materials in a manufacturing facility. They need a solid set of guiding ideas that will enable the team to create a project plan. Backcasting will help them form a vision of how the product should work and the basic principles it should reflect.

Collect Existing Research: Begin by collecting the previous research. For this team some recent interviews with stakeholders provide helpful details.

Brainstorm Future States: As a team, use the initial research to form ideas about what the final product could look like. Consider multiple future states that could happen.

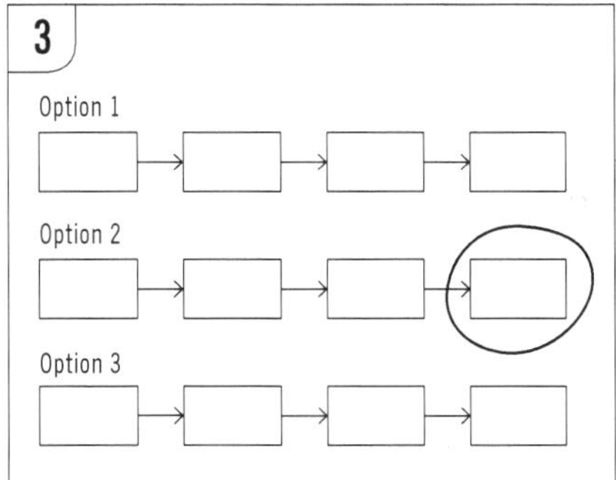

Agree on the Vision: As a team select an end state to aim for and set this as the long term goal.

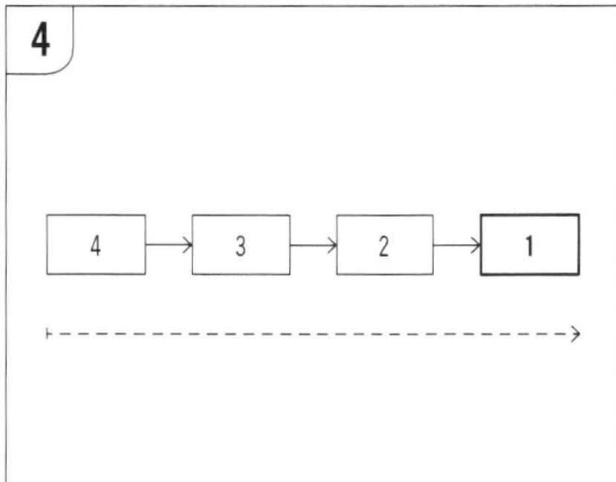

Form a Plan: Create a detailed plan by working backwards from the desired future state.

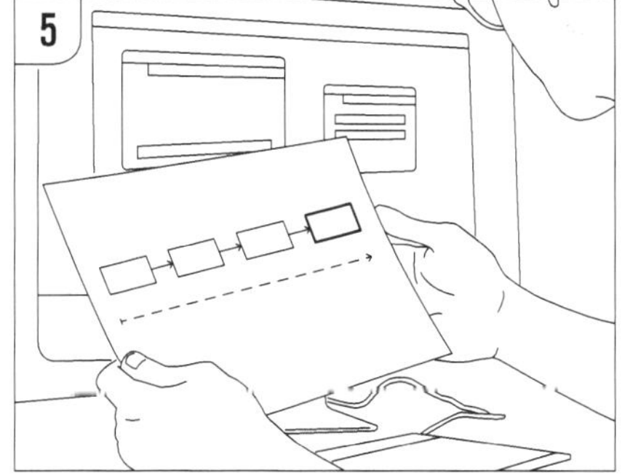

Use the Vision: As the product is being built, reference the vision to make sure that the product is moving towards the established goal. Course correct the team as needed.

Bodystorming

Bodystorming is a physical role-playing method where the participant acts as a user to gain an empathetic view on environmental scenarios and experiences.

First, define the tasks and goals that the participants will play out. Either visit or recreate the environment that needs to be tested. Physically go through the scenario from start to finish. The major aspect that separates this method from others is the true investment into physical role-playing that is used to discover information about the experience. This can be done alone, or a team could do the task together and observe the other team members.

Depending on the type of task being performed, it can also be helpful to play out physical restrictions a user might have. For example, consider how your product might be used by a person in a wheelchair, by someone with poor vision, by a parent distracted by children or by someone who simply has a major distraction. These types of restraints can easily be experienced by the researcher and provide fresh insight into the user's experience.

When to use: When environmental factors have a strong role in the use of a product and an empathetic view is needed.

Difficulty: Average   **Time:** 1 Day   **Participants:** 1+

Bodystorming Example

In this example a home automation system is being tested. The designer wants to see how well a function to open the blinds works. The bodystorming method helps experience the product in the same way as users by recreating the physical environment.

Establish the Environment: For this example the experience will begin when the participant wakes up.

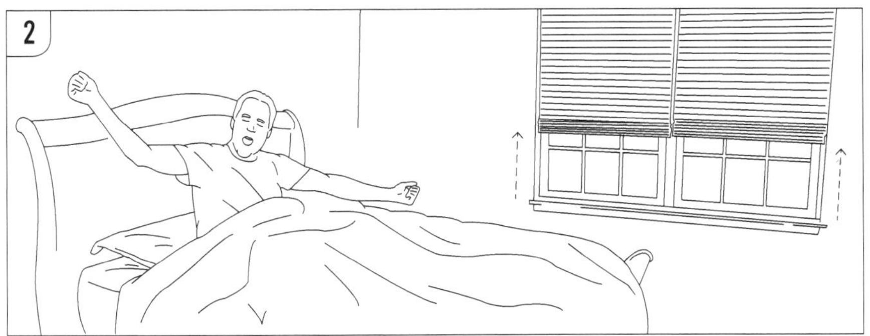

Simulate the Experience: Next, the participant recreates waking up in the morning and gives the verbal command to "open shades" in the bedroom. Simulate this by having someone pulling the shades up on command.

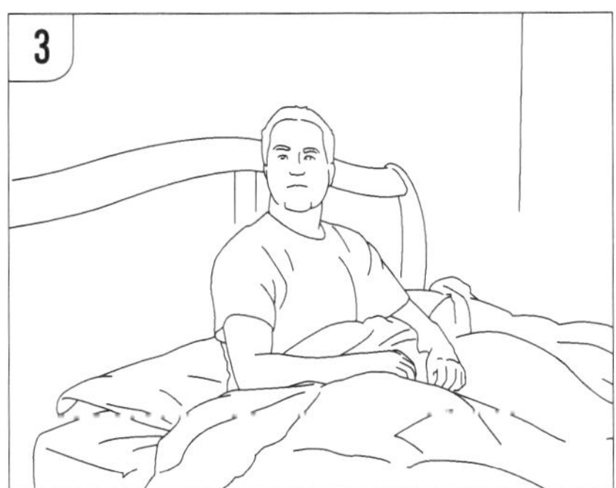

Observe Details: As the participant goes through the experience, take note of details you previously overlooked.

Review Observation: Meet with your team to discuss what you learned and how it might impact the design.

Business Origami

Business origami is when paper cutouts are used to examine the components of a system and their potential interactions and relationships.

Start by creating cutouts of all the systems components (people, locations, data points, etc.) and place them on a whiteboard or tabletop. Participants then move the components around the board and draw the relationships within the system and experience. When the desired interactions are established, they can be refined into a digital representation. Use a photograph to make sure and capture the results.

This method can be used to visualize how physical and digital elements might become interconnected. It can also work as a sort of tangible flow charting. The physical nature of the method forces the team to really talk about how the elements relate to each other and how the interactions for the user might be optimized. This can lead to a shared vision for the project.

When to use: After user research has produced a divergent set of possibilities and a solution has not yet been identified.

Difficulty: Easy　　　　**Time:** 4 Hours　　　　**Participants:** 5+

Business Origami Example

In this example a new check-in system for a conference needs to be created. They want to see the most optimal way for attendees to get their tickets and pick up secondary supplies. This method will allow the design team to quickly run through multiple scenarios and visualize the results with minimal time investment.

Create Components: Using printouts or drawn elements on paper, create people, objects and physical structures that are involved in the process.

Explore Relationships within System: On a large table, work with the team to move the components around and discuss relationships of the user experiences.

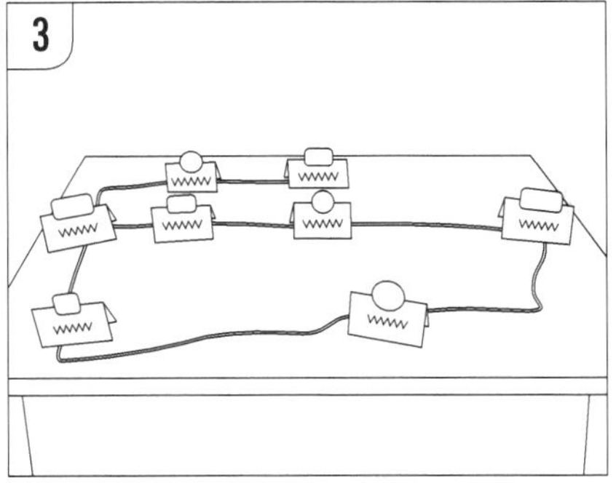

Draw Paths of Interaction: Using string or other tools, plot out paths showing how users would move and interact with elements at the conference.

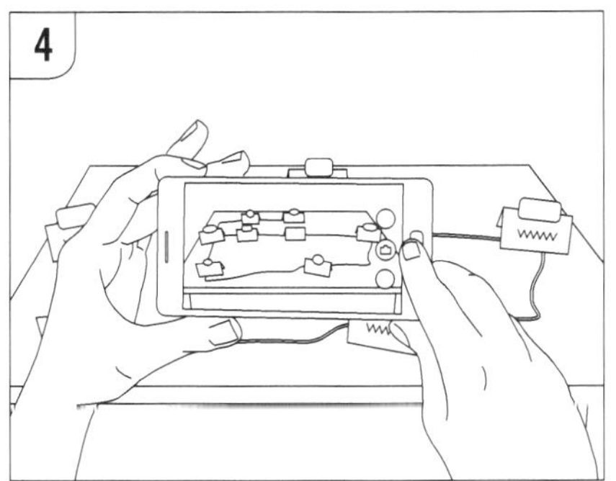

Repeat Exploration and Discussion: Once one scenario is established, take a photo to capture the idea. Repeat the exploration and discuss another scenario.

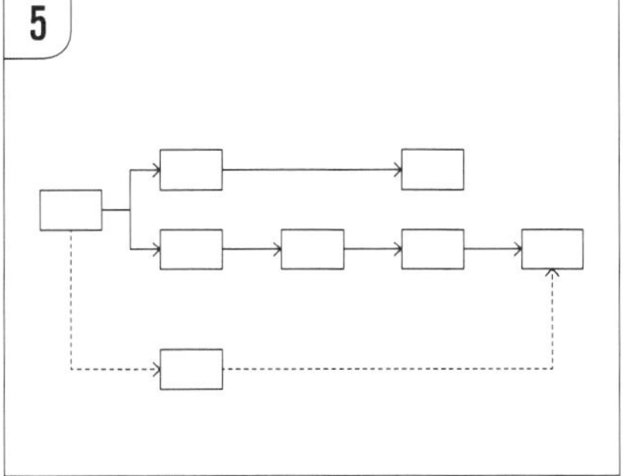

Create Digital Representation: Once a suitable approach has been found, create a digital version so other stakeholders can reference and use the plan.

Card Sorting

Use a card sort to define your content structure based on an understanding of how users expect your content to be organized.

To begin, write the title for each section of content onto an index card. Ask a potential user to sort these cards into groups based on how they would organize them. Next, ask the user to create a title for each grouping they defined.

Have a second user come in and review how the cards were organized by the previous participant. Ask them to make any modifications to the structure. The user can add new groups or relocate cards. Make note of cards that get moved. Repeat this revision process with at least 3–5 additional users.

When done, you can review where the cards ended up and have a good idea of how users expect your content to be organized. Cards that were moved frequently can indicate content that might be difficult for users to find.

Note that this form of card sort doesn't fit the traditional open and closed methods frequently described. It relies on a single result that multiple participants help to form. This makes it a much simpler method to implement.

When to use: When you have a large amount of content to organize.

Difficulty: Average   **Time:** 4 Hours   **Participants:** 5+

Card Sorting Example

In this example the team is unsure how to organize a large library of videos. There are multiple ways it could be organized. A card sort will help the designer discover how users will expect the content to be organized.

Prepare the Cards: Select a small set of samples including each type of video content. The title of each is written on a card.

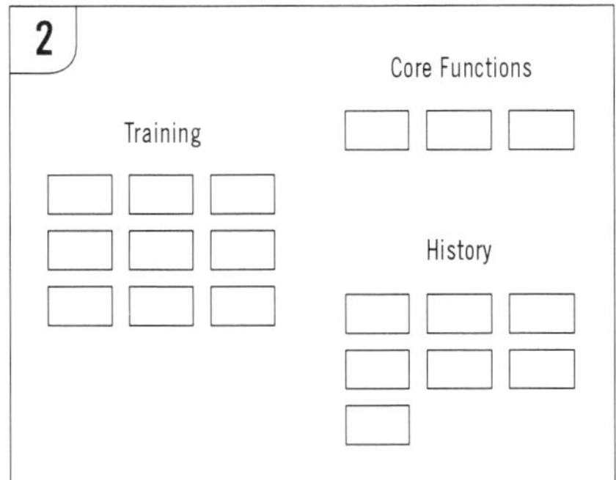

Sort Cards: The first participant is asked to sort the cards into groups as they would expect them to be organized and gives each grouping a title.

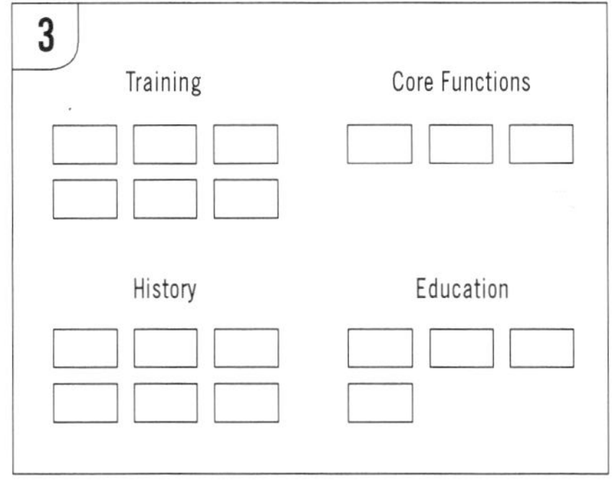

Continue Sorting: After the first participant leaves, another participant is asked to modify the previous participants work in any way they want. Repeat this with at least 4 additional participants.

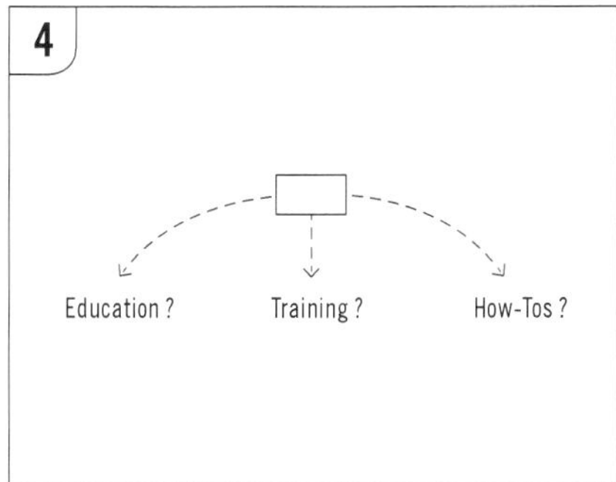

Observe Sorting: As each participant manipulates the cards, pay attention to ones that are frequently relocated; this is content that users will likely look for in multiple places.

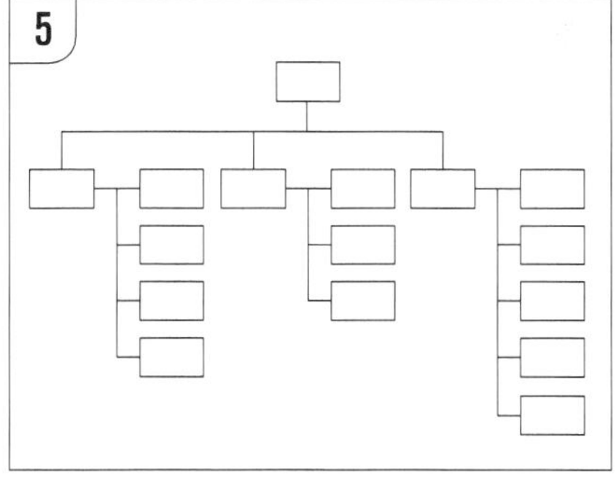

Review Results: Now the team has a structure for the videos that reflects users expectations.

Method Reference: http://uxpajournal.org/a-modified-delphi-approach-to-a-new-card-sorting-methodology/, November 2008, by Celeste Lyn Paul.

Claims Analysis

Claims analysis is used to assess a variety of ideas in order to identify positive and negative effects it might have.

First, determine the key feature(s) that are going to be examined along with a claim about the effect of the possible change. List the positive and negative attributes of the new features; make sure you take into consideration the users and key stakeholders. One option is to place positive claims on one form of visual notation and negative claims on a different kind so that they can be placed around the feature to get a visual snapshot of the overall analysis. When multiple claims analyses are complete, you can compare the results of each to form priorities.

This is a useful method when team members cannot agree on how to proceed. Oftentimes it is difficult to see past certain benefits or roadblocks of an idea. By writing down the positive and negative aspects, team members can move beyond those key details they are stuck on. By viewing all of the ideas, and the good and bad qualities of each, arguments can often be resolved.

When to use: When new features are being debated and a consensus is needed.

Difficulty: Average　　　　　**Time:** 1 Hour　　　　　**Participants:** 5+

Claims Analysis Example

In this example the team is debating multiple features to improve the usability of a mobile game. Based on the user feedback there are many possible features, all of which have good and bad qualities. Using a claims analysis the team can gain a better understanding of the options and which ones might be good to implement.

Identify the Key Features: As a team start by listing features being considered on a whiteboard.

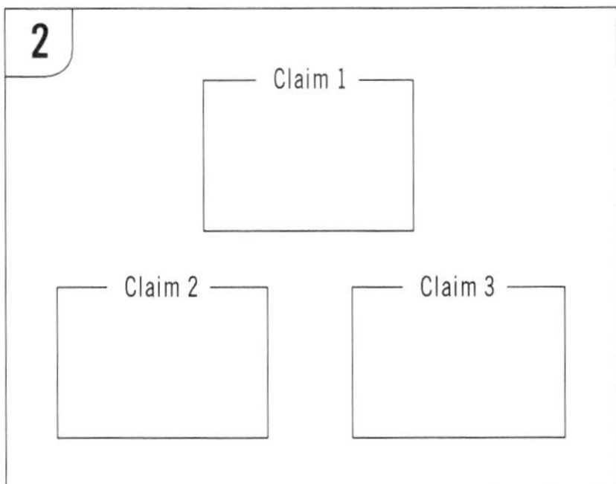

Collect Claims: The team collects all of the claims about each feature and prepares them for review. A claim could be "adding a scoring feature would improve player engagement."

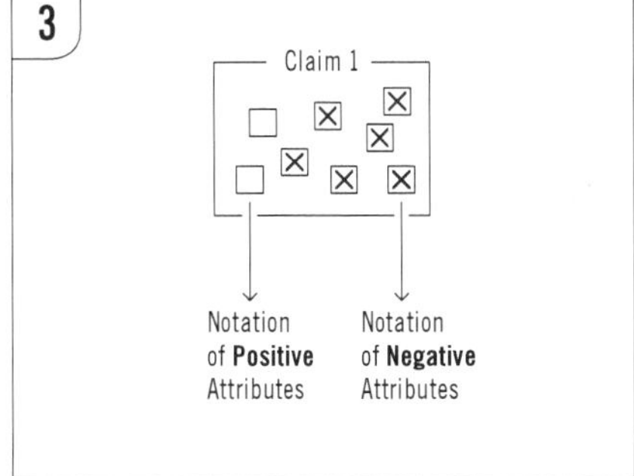

Review and Rate Claims: List all of the positive and negative attributes for each claim. Use a strong visual element to distinguish the positive from the negative.

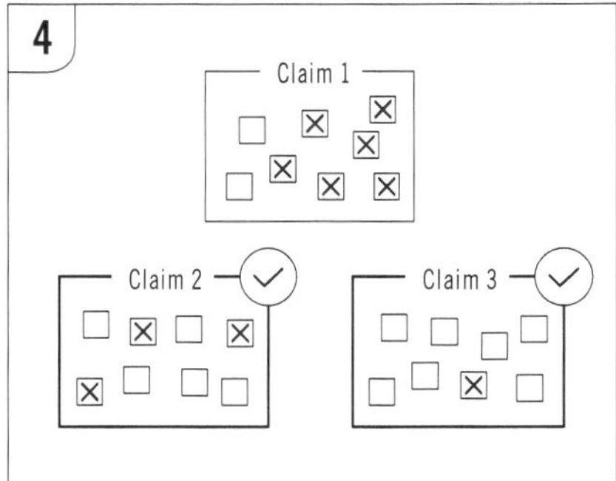

Discuss and Identify: With all of the facts collected the team is able to discuss the features and identify which options might be the best choice.

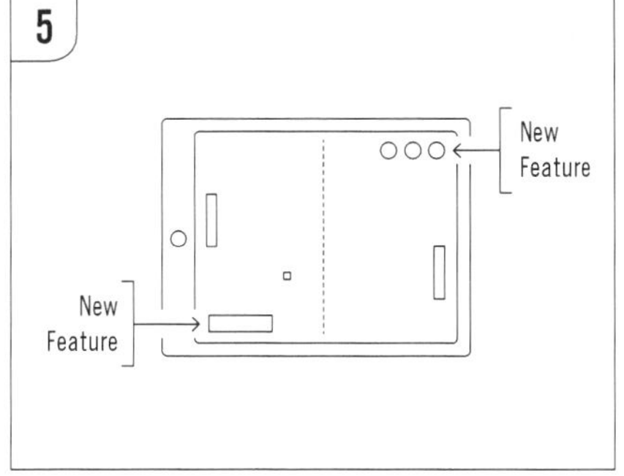

Assess the Results: The team is able to make an informed choice about which new features to pursue and how to prioritize their work.

Cognitive Walkthrough

The cognitive walkthrough is used to identify usability issues by stepping through a task and considering the user's perspective at each step.

To begin a cognitive walkthrough you must first define the specific tasks you want to test within your product. Keep in mind, this method is not intended to assess a system as a whole, but rather specific tasks.

Next, assemble a group of team members with a mix of perspectives such as developers, designers, project managers, accountants or anyone else available. The ideal group would have someone representing the user and would include at least one person not intimately familiar with the product.

Walk through each step and ask the following questions as outlined by Polson Blackmon in *Cognitive Walkthrough for the Web*:
1. Will the user try and achieve the right outcome?
2. Will the user notice that the correct action is available to them?
3. Will the user associate the correct action with the outcome they expect to achieve?
4. If the correct action is performed, will the user see that progress is being made towards their intended outcome?

When to use: To see if a specific task is easily understood, discovered and used.

Difficulty: Hard   **Time:** 1 Hour   **Participants:** 5+

Cognitive Walkthrough Example

In this example the team is designing a new system for customers to report lost and stolen credit cards. The team needs to look at the system from a user's perspective but doesn't have the time or budget to set up a full usability test. The cognitive walkthrough enables them to look at things from the user's perspective and get them much needed feedback.

Define Tasks: The team begins by documenting the tasks they want to test. Ex: A customer is on vacation and has to report a lost credit card on their phone.

Assemble the Team: A team with mixed perspectives is assembled, including someone specifically representing the user.

Conduct the Walkthrough: As a group the team walks through each step of the task considering each of the four predefined questions (on page 22).

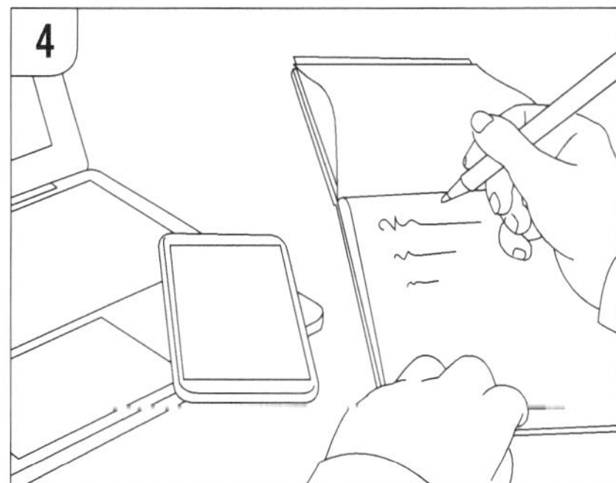

Track the Results: During the walkthrough take notes to ensure the team captures the results of each step.

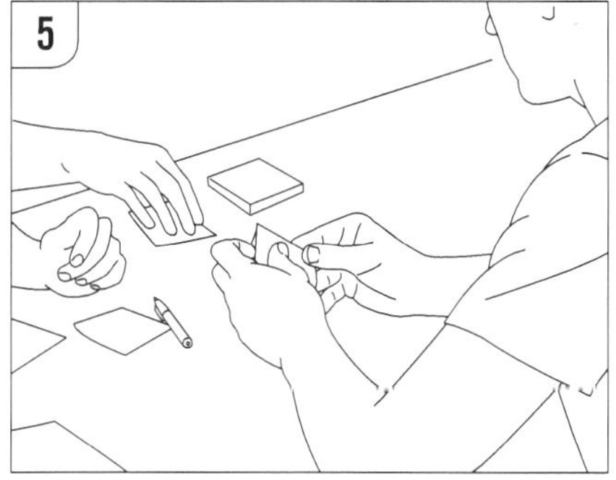

Interpret Results: The team can now continue to move the project forward knowing they have a user's perspective influencing their design.

Method Reference: Blackmon, M. H. Polson, P.G. Muneo, K & Lewis, C. (2002) *Cognitive Walkthrough for the Web.* CHI 2002 vol.4 No.1 pg 463–470.

Competitive Analysis

Use a competitive analysis to understand how your product compares to your competitors' products.

To begin a competitive analysis you must select the type (or types) of comparison you will be conducting. Types of comparison include features, usability, visual styles, content structure, interface type, price point, optional features and so on. Create a table with each attribute you will compare as a separate row.

Next, research the market to identify the competitors you will be analyzing. In the table create a column for each product (including your own) that you will be comparing. In each box describe how each product satisfies that topic. As you add data to the grid, note in each cell if the results are good, bad or neutral. You can create a more detailed scale if needed. Color coding can also be very helpful.

Finally, assess the results and make a concise list of recommendations including the following:
- Your products' unique strengths that should be emphasized
- Your products' competitive weaknesses that might be addressed
- Strengths in competitors' products that represent threats
- Weaknesses in competitors' products that represent opportunities

When to use: When you need to identify ways to make your product stand out in the market.

Difficulty: Average   **Time:** 1 Hour   **Participants:** 5+

Competitive Analysis Example

A team has been tasked with finding ways to enhance a small business accounting application to make it more competitive and to fuel growth of the customer base. The team needs to better understand how the competition stacks up and what opportunities might exist in the market. A competitive analysis will help them systematically compare their product to the competition.

1

Mobile Interface

Usability

Point of Sale Integration

Integrations and Connectivity

Plan the Topics: First, the team must list what aspects they will be comparing.

2

	Product 1	Product 2	Product 3
Mobile Interface			
Point of Sale Integration			
Integrations and Connectivity			

List the Competition: The team creates a list of products they will compare their product to. These are placed into a matrix with each topic in a row and each product as a column.

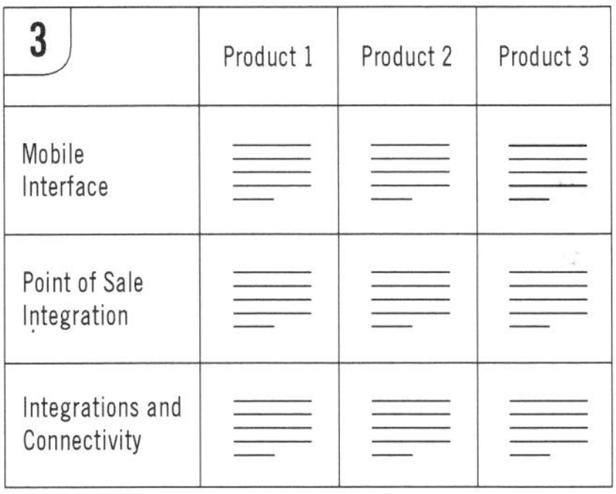

3

	Product 1	Product 2	Product 3
Mobile Interface			
Point of Sale Integration			
Integrations and Connectivity			

Conduct the Analysis: Each product is investigated and notes are added to the matrix for each product on each topic. Each cell of the grid is color coded based on the agreed upon scale.

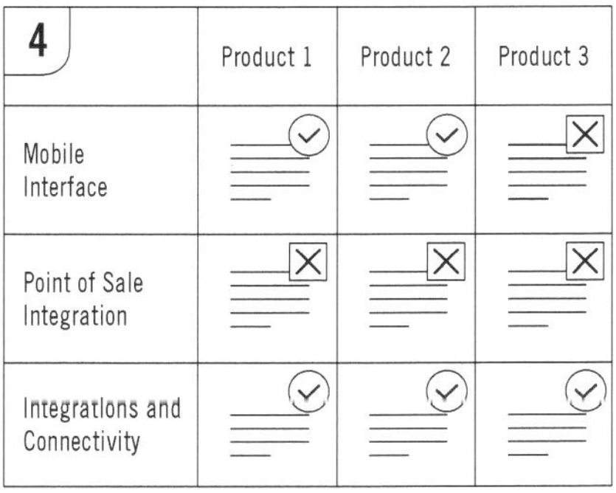

4

	Product 1	Product 2	Product 3
Mobile Interface	✓	✓	✗
Point of Sale Integration	✗	✗	✗
Integrations and Connectivity	✓	✓	✓

Create Coding System: Mark or color code the grid to reflect how effectively each product addresses the topics being reviewed.

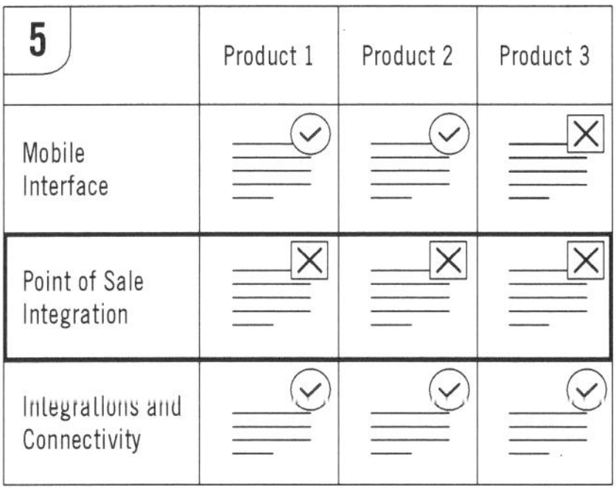

5

	Product 1	Product 2	Product 3
Mobile Interface	✓	✓	✗
Point of Sale Integration	✗	✗	✗
Integrations and Connectivity	✓	✓	✓

Conduct Further Research: Now that the team sees the holes in the market they can conduct additional research with users to discover if these represent opportunities for the software to expand into.

Concept Model Process

The concept model process is a method used to understand the relationships between all of the components within a subject domain through a visualization.

A concept model is built using ovals with nouns inside and arrows with verbs on them. The combination of noun-verb-noun creates a sort of sentence describing how two elements relate to each other.

To get started, break the topic down into the elements that make up the problem area; these are the nouns. Place each noun into circles (or ovals). Connect a noun to another noun with a one-way arrow. Put a verb on the arrow. When read aloud, in the direction of the arrow, you should get a noun-verb-noun sentence. Repeat this to connect as many of the nouns as possible to each other.

When finished, your diagram will provide a full view of all the elements in the subject area and should have many connections showing how they are all related to each other. In some cases you will want to add a key to further explain the elements of the diagram. Most often a concept model is made for the research team and is not typically shared with other stakeholders. This mapping helps the team consider relationships not previously observed.

When to use: When a subject area is too complex to immediately understand.

Difficulty: Average   **Time:** 1 Hour   **Participants:** 0

Concept Model Process Example

A design team has been tasked with finding ways to use technology to engage visitors to a large theme park. First, the team needs to understand the complex inter relationships of all the interaction points visitors have. This includes both physical and digital. A concept model will help them create a visual representation of these elements and how they relate to each other.

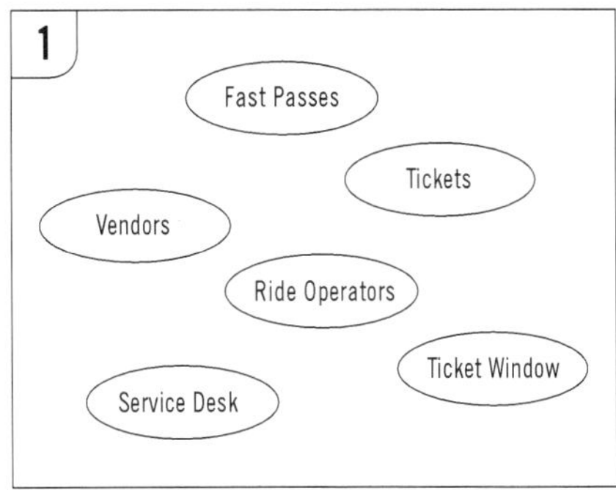

List Elements: To begin the team lists all of the elements and interaction points (nouns) that are part of the theme park and places each into an oval.

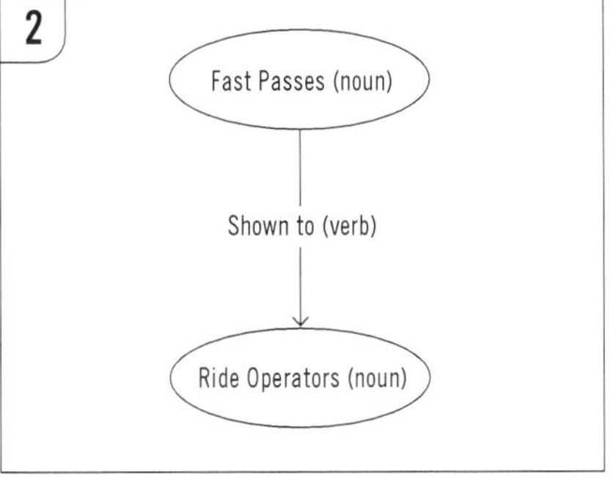

Make Connections: Connect nouns to each other using an arrow pointing one direction, putting verbs on each line such that the noun-verb-noun combination creates a sentence.

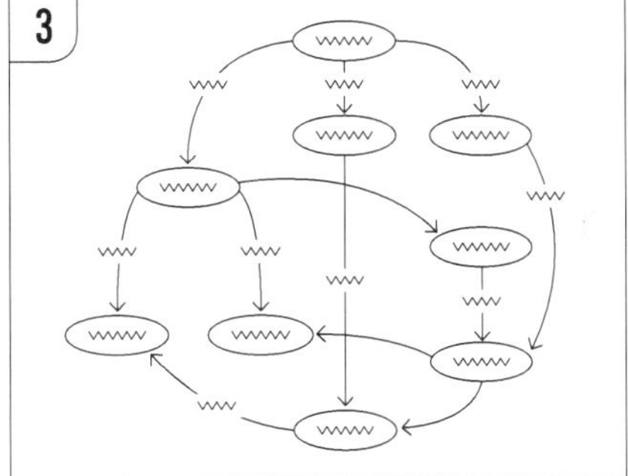

Continue Connections: Continue to make as many connections as possible. At first connections are obvious; move beyond this to find deeper, less apparent relationships.

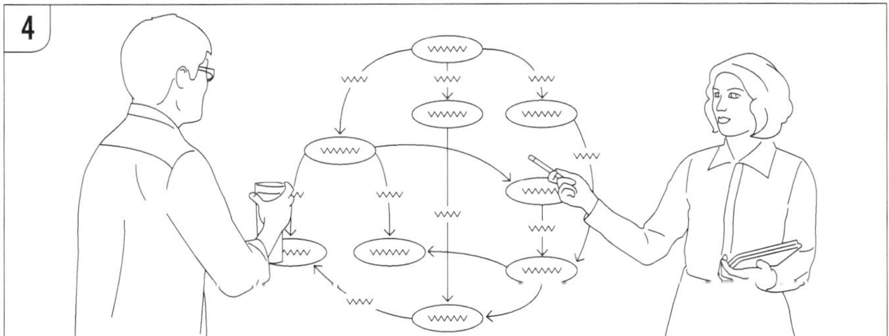

Review and Discuss: Together the team reviews the diagram and discusses the relationships and unexpected connections. The team has a much better understanding of the topic now and is able to brainstorm ideas that they might further explore.

Contextual Inquiry

Contextual inquiry is a research method conducted by visiting users in their natural setting and observing how they use your product.

With contextual inquiry you visit your users to observe them as they use your product in a natural setting. Begin by talking to the user in order to build trust with them. Reinforce that your goal is to observe them as they use your product. Reassure them that you are not there to assess them or their performance. A good approach is to say something like "I am here to figure out how we can improve our product to make it easier for you to use." This gets the user out of the mindset that they are being scrutinized. Once you have established a connection with the user ask them to perform their work as normal.

At natural stopping points during the observation and at the end you can ask follow-up questions. Ask about why they did certain things, or what they were trying to accomplish at certain points. Or even how they were feeling during key steps.

Contextual inquiry is often confused with field studies (page 40). Note that in a contextual inquiry you are specifically watching users with your product. In contrast a field study is to watch the user work in general and to discover ways to help them.

When to use: To eliminate assumptions about how your product is being used.

Difficulty: Average   **Time:** 1 day   **Participants:** 5+

Contextual Inquiry Example

A service company with field technicians has a custom mobile app for its employees that is very underutilized. The team needs to understand how the app is being used, and what the technicians' work actually looks like. contextual inquiry will help them discover this information and find ways the app might be improved to increase utilization.

Visit the Users: Pair up with technicians and travel with them as they work for one day.

Take Notes: Throughout the day take notes on how the user works, what types of tasks they do, and note ideas for how an app might make their job easier.

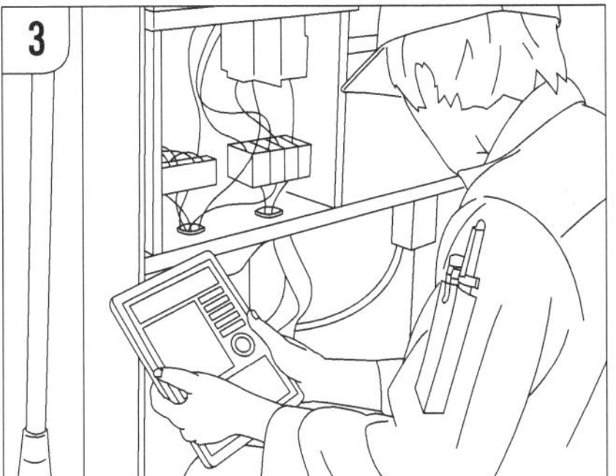

Repeat: Repeat this with several different users to get a wide range of perspectives.

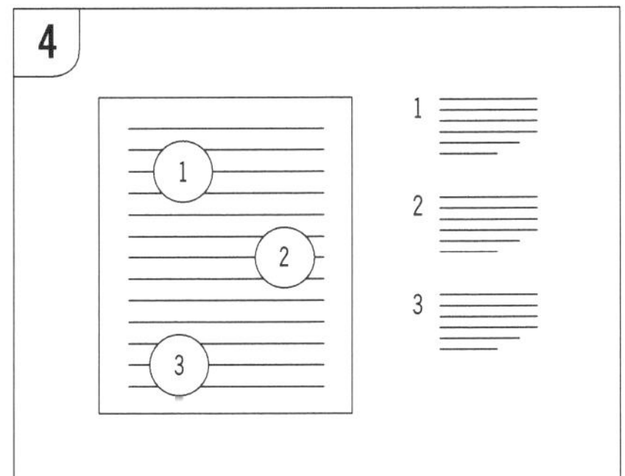

Collect Results: After the fieldwork is done the team collects all of their findings and sorts them into groups or patterns.

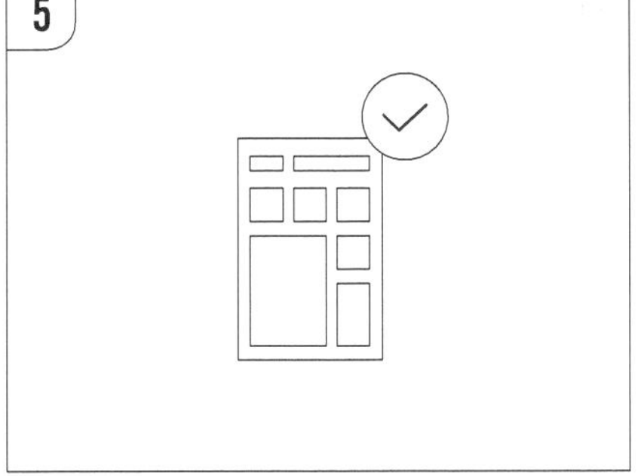

Interpret the Results: With real insight into how the field techs are working the team is able to propose significant changes to the application that will have a much greater impact on the usage of the app.

Method Reference: Blackmon, M. H. Polson, P.G. Muneo, K & Lewis, C. (2002) *Cognitive Walkthrough for the Web* CHI 2002 vol.4 No.1 pg 463–470.

Desirability Studies

Desirability studies are when variations of visual designs are shown to a participant and they are asked to make an association from a word list so that a better understanding of emotional response can be understood.

Start by preparing a list of adjectives that connect the brand to the designs that will be tested. Half the words should have a desirable association and the other half should be negative. Mix the words together in a random order. It is recommended that the list contain 30–50 words.

Print out multiple design variations and post them to a whiteboard or wall. Ask each participant to select 3–5 words from the list that they associate with each design. Repeat this with at least 5 participants. Assemble the results and look for patterns in the words participants are using to describe each design.

If you have time, it is preferred to have 5 different participants for each design variation. The more similar the design options are, the more important it is that each design is tested with separate users.

When to use: When multiple variations of a visual design are being considered.

Difficulty: Easy　　　　　　**Time:** 4 Hours　　　　　　**Participants:** 5+

Desirability Studies Example

In this example the visual brand of a homepage is being updated. Variations of homepage designs are being created and the most desirable version needs to be discovered. This method is useful to track responses and make a decision based on the project's goals.

Create Word List: Create a list of positive and negative adjectives that have an association with the new brand.

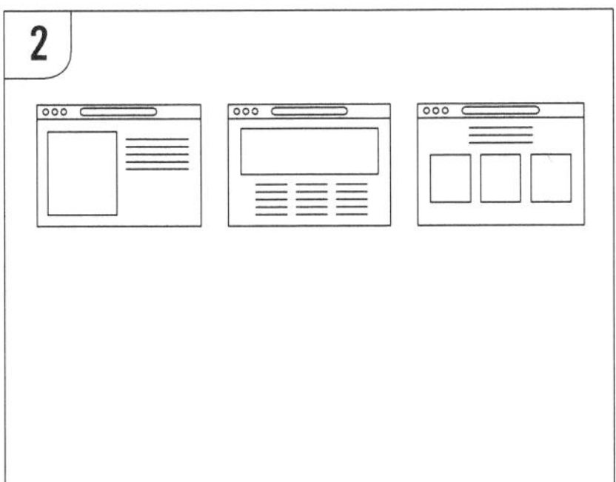

Display Visual Designs: Display the homepage designs (in a medium of your choice) for the participant to review.

Review Visual Designs: Ask the participant to review the designs and select words from the provided list that they associate with each design.

Observe Participant: Make notes of the words that each participant chooses for each design and repeat as needed.

Interpret Results: Look for patterns to help you decide which version best reflects the new brand.

Method Reference: http://www.uxmatters.com/mt/archives/2010/02/rapid-desirability-testing-a-case-study.php, February 22, 2010, by Michael Hawley

Elito Method

Elito method is when research observations are gathered into a spreadsheet and further examined in a structured way.

Start by creating a spreadsheet with a column for observations, judgement, value, concept, key metaphors, and extra. Each observation will be placed on a separate row.

Observations: Individual observations about the user experience.

Judgement: An explanation or interpretation of the observation.

Value (motivation): The importance or usefulness of the observation for the user.

Concept/sketch: Describe a solution based on the information related to this observation.

Key Metaphor: A short phase that can act as a figure of speech for the observation.

Extra - Place and Topic: Single-word summaries of the observation. These can be useful later when sorting the results.

As a team, review one observation at a time and fill out each cell of the grid. This forces the team to systematically consider each observation.

When to use: Right after initial research has been completed and it is unclear how to execute on the results.

Difficulty: Very Hard   **Time:** 1 Day   **Participants:** 1+

Elito Method Example

A team has already observed employees in a customer service call center in order to find ways to reduce call length. They collected many observations and discovered that the workflows are far more complicated than expected. The team is unsure how to interpret their findings. The Elito method will help them organize and examine the results in a structured way.

Build the Spreadsheet: Create a spreadsheet with six columns. One each for observations, judgement, value, concept, key metaphor and extra.

2

	A
	Observations
1	Users have to re-enter the customer's name in multiple systems.
2	Agents interpret information in different ways and frequently make assumptions about the caller's situation.
3	Agents use numerous, self-created utilities to answer many questions.

Add Observations: Add all of the observations to the first column. Each row should contain a distinct observation.

3

	B
	Judgement
	This can lead to errors.
	Customers get different answers and inconsistent service.
	This makes it difficult to train new staff.

Complete the Examination: Work through all of the observations and fill in the remainder of the cells (per the instructions on page 32).

Interpret Results: The team now has a much better understanding of the importance of certain observations and is able to identify the most important elements to work on.

Emoticon Score Method

The emoticon score is a Likert style scale used to rate the likeability of something.

First, create the emoticon scale. This should be a 5-step scale going from extremely negative to extremely positive. Though participants don't see the number, assign the numbers 1 through 5 to each point on the chart, 1 being the most negative.

Next, write the question to your users. Use the format "What do you think of _____?" or "How did you feel about _____?" The blank will be filled in by the participant.

After a user completes the task being studied, present them with the question and emoticon scale. The user selects the emoticon that best answers the question for them.

To interpret the results average the score. This number can be used to assess the overall likeability or emotional response to the feature and can be used to compare versions of a feature or a system over time.

Note that the emoticon method can be used on live products or on prototypes. The method can be done digitally or even on paper.

When to use: When you need to understand the users' emotional reaction to something.

Difficulty: Very Easy　　　　**Time:** 1 Hour　　　　**Participants:** 5+

Emoticon Score Method Example

Changes to a digital checkout system are being developed. They want to see if the modified experience works and is enjoyable for the user. This method works well because users can respond quickly and the resulting data is on a quantifiable scale.

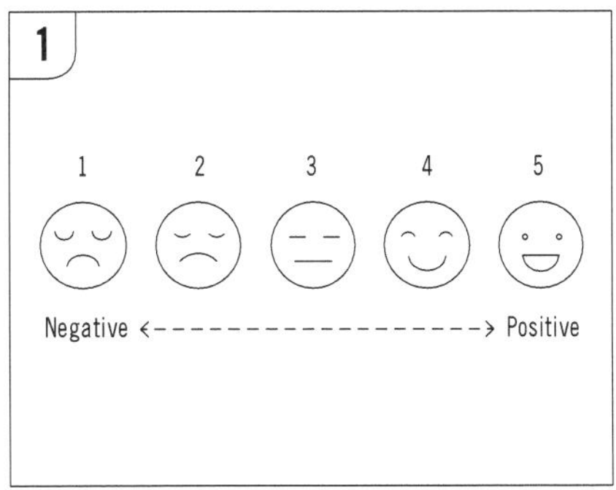

Develop Visuals: Determine the visual forms of the emoticons, starting with the negative on the left (1) to the positive (5) on the right.

Form Question: Write a question based on the experience you are evaluating and place it above the emoticon score. In this case "What do you think of the checkout experience?"

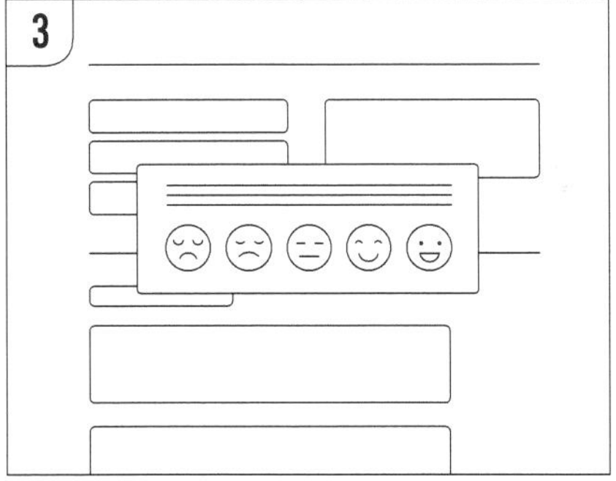

Collect Data: After the user has used the digital checkout system, have the emoticon scale and question appear so that the user can take part in the method.

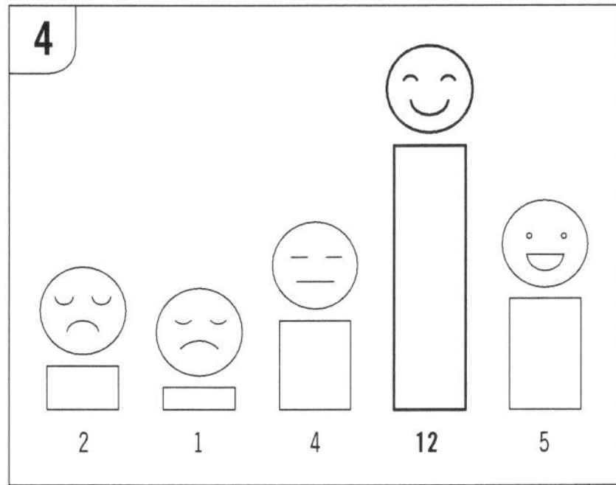

Chart Results: After enough data is collected, use the scoring system (1 - 5) to tally the results and see if users "like" the new checkout process.

Iterate on the Design: The team can continue to modify the system and repeat this method. By comparing test data they can understand if they are improving the system.

Empathy Interview

Empathy-based interviews are informal conversations where the goal is to understand a person's motivations and feelings.

Start an empathy interview anytime you're talking to someone and want to learn about something. Ask the person lots of open-ended questions. Allow the conversation to flow, but gently guide it back to the topic you're interested in. Keep the focus on the other person and resist the temptation to talk about yourself. Use this to discover how the person feels and what they care about. In the end, the person won't even know they have been interviewed. After the interview, and out of view of the participant, jot down notes about what you learned.

Typically you don't plan to have an empathy interview; it's more like something you do when you happen to have the opportunity. An empathy-based interview differs from a traditional interview in that there are no questions prepared ahead of time. That said, here are some great questions to get people to talk more:

- How does that make you feel?
- What do you like/dislike about that?
- Tell me more about that.

When to use: When you need to learn about people and create divergent thinking.

Difficulty: Average　　　　　**Time:** 30 Minutes　　　　　**Participants:** 1+

Empathy Interview Example

An individual is researching how parents interact with their children's teachers at school. Recently she was at a party and was sitting next to a parent of several children. The empathy interview is perfect for this situation as it allows the individual to gather data in an unstructured and informal way.

Start a Conversation: The researcher simply starts talking to the parent, striking up a conversation about the other individual's children.

Ask Questions: The parent is talkative, so the researcher continues to ask questions. She allows the conversation to flow naturally, but at times she does ask questions related to her research topic.

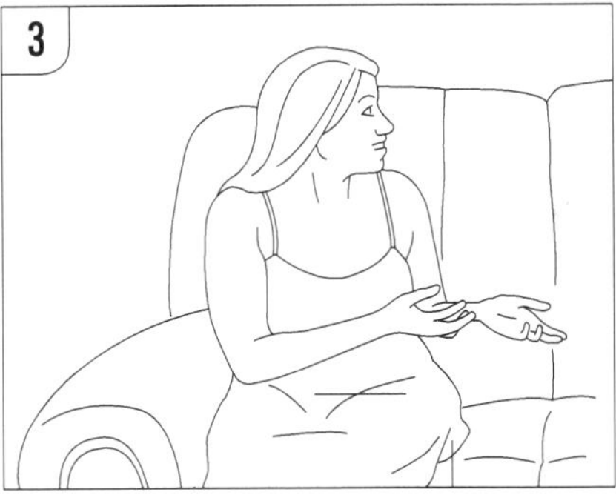

Listen: The researcher fights the natural instinct to talk about oneself. This keeps the participant talking.

Research Stealthily: The participant doesn't even have to know that they were just interviewed. It just felt like a good conversation, because people like to talk about themselves.

Archive Feedback Immediately: After the conversation is over, the researcher jots down memorable notes that relate to the research topic.

Empathy Map

The empathy map examines users' thoughts and feelings by asking questions based on a four quadrant diagram to help understand their motivations and decisions.

On a whiteboard, draw a four quadrant diagram with a head in the center; this reinforces that we are talking about a real person. Write out the following questions in the four quadrants:

- What does the user Say? (Explicit - things you see)
- What does the user Do? (Explicit)
- What does the user Think? (Implicit - things you don't see)
- What does the user Feel? (Implicit)

Start with the explicit half, these are the exact things the user says and does. Using sticky notes, write down a quote the user said about the research topic and post it to the "Say" section. Next, post what the users actually do in the "Do" section. For the implicit quadrants, start by writing down what you believe they are thinking in the "Think" section. Next, write down what you believe they are feeling in the "Feel" section.

Two optional sections can also be added:

- Pain (Problems): What is standing in their way?
- Gain (Goals): What do they want to accomplish?

When to use: Early in the process after you have observed or interviewed users.

Difficulty: Hard   **Time:** 1 Hour   **Participants:** 5+

Empathy Map Example

An auto dealership wants to set themselves apart in the market by radically changing the car purchasing experience. The team wants to gain a deep understanding of the customers' thoughts and feelings as a foundation to build on. The empathy map provides a structured way to collect and present this type of data.

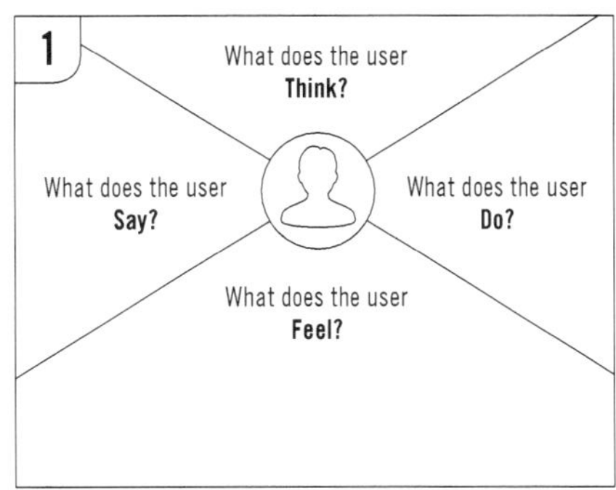

Set Up the Diagram: Using a large whiteboard the team sets up the four quadrant diagram as described in the text on page 38.

Observe Customers: The team observes customers at their dealerships, taking notes based on the four main questions on page 38.

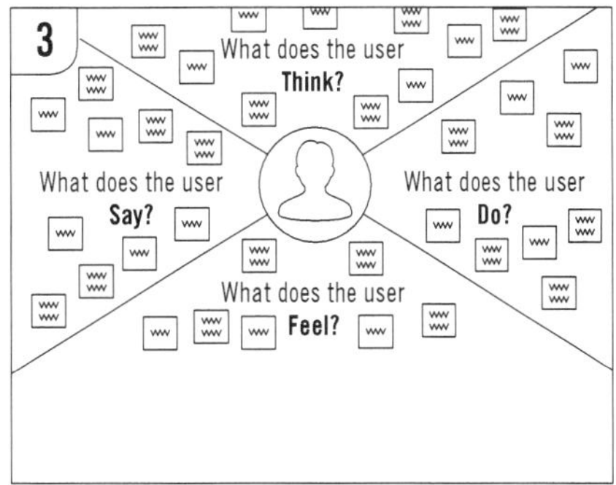

Collect Results: The resulting data is posted on the large diagram using Post-it notes.

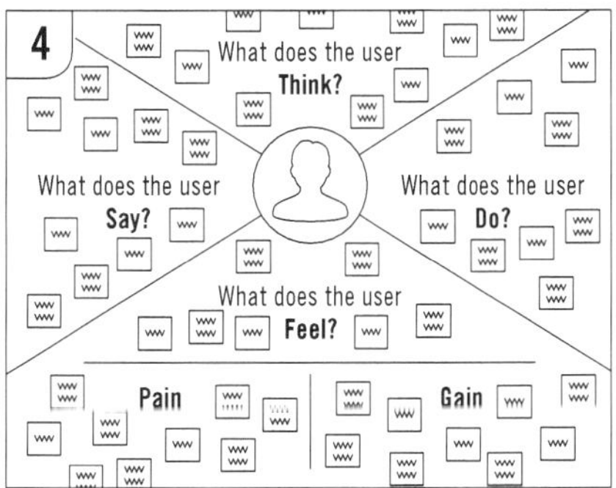

Expand on the Results: The team adds the Pains and Gains section to the diagram and fills it with notes based on their customer observations.

5

Customers will price shop so we should embrace it.

Upgrade packages are confusing

Having all the cars locked slows the shopper from trying them out.

Evaluate: Using the diagram the team is able to identify the most prominent dynamics that need to be changed and can put plans together for how to improve the experience.

Field Studies

Field studies are when a researcher goes where users are in order to directly observe them in a natural environment.

Determine times when the user is actually going through an experience. Let them know that you will be observing them so they are not surprised. Observe the user and take note of your observations as they work through an experience. After observing a user a follow-up interview can help you gain understanding about the behaviors, goals and feelings the participant had while completing the task.

Field studies seek to discover how users are behaving in a natural setting. In contrast, contextual inquiry (page 28) is interested in discovering how your product is being used. Use a field study when you want to discover problems you can help users with and a contextual inquiry when you want to see how your product is actually used.

Depending on your goals a field study can also be done without talking to the user or notifying them that you are observing them. If the setting allows you can simply watch and take notes.

When to use: To get a firsthand understanding of what the user is experiencing and what problems they are facing.

Difficulty: Average   **Time:** 1 Day   **Participants:** 1+

Field Studies Example

A shopping mall wants to improve the overall customer experience in order to better compete with online shopping. The team needs to understand how customers behave in order to propose improvements. A field study will allow the team to gain big-picture insights about the customer experience and directly observe their natural behaviors.

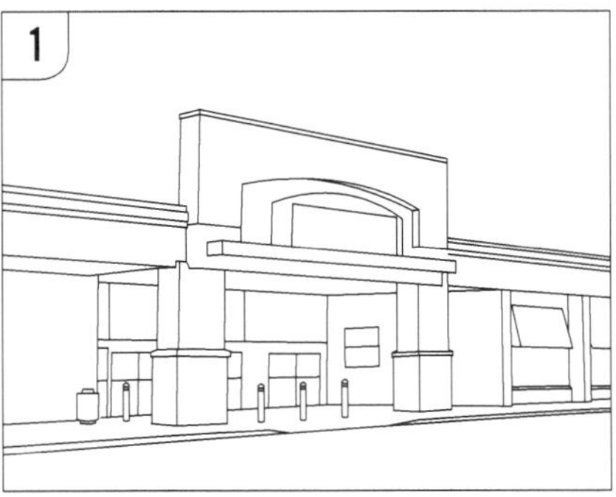

Plan the Visit: The team suspects that different types of customers visit at different times of day and plan five 4-hour visits to observe users at different times.

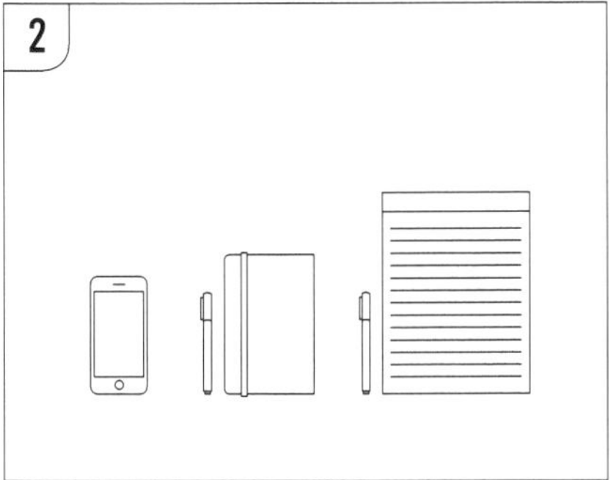

Bring Tools: During the visit the team brings notebooks and their digital devices so they can capture photos and videos.

Observation and Take Notes: The team observes the customers, taking notes on behaviors, customer demographics and other relevant details.

Debrief: After each site visit the team meets to discuss their findings while the experience is fresh.

Summarize Results: At the end of the field studies the team is able to summarize their experience and findings about the audience into a clear list of important items. This helps guide the team's next steps.

First Click Test

The first click test is used to discover if users can effectively find the first step towards accomplishing some goal in an interface.

Get started by printing your design in wireframe or hi-fidelity format. Present the design to each user and ask them to circle where they would click to start a given task. Repeat this with approximately 5 users to see how frequently people correctly identify where to go in the design. Based on the results adjust your design and repeat the process.

If you want to take this to the next level there are online tools where you can upload your designs and run the test online with users around the world.

Research shows that when a user's first click to achieve a task is down a correct path they have an 87 percent chance of completing the task. In contrast users whose first click is down an incorrect path only have a 46 percent chance of completing the task. In simpler terms, a correct first click towards the goal nearly doubles the chances of completing the task.

When to use: To test if you have made a feature visible enough.

Difficulty: Easy   **Time:** 1 Hour   **Participants:** 5+

First Click Test Example

A new product category of sleep tracking devices is being added to an ecommerce site. The team is unsure how to label this new section and is worried users will not know how to find it. The team decides to use a first click test as it will help them make sure users can correctly navigate to the new section.

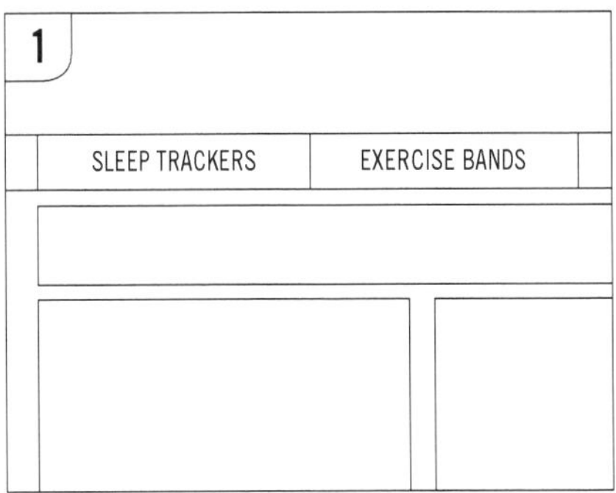

Prepare the Prototype: The team creates a prototype to simulate the task users will be asked to perform.

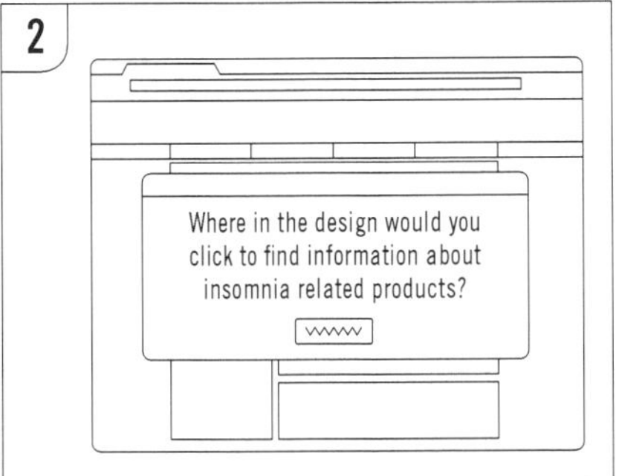

Plan the Task: The task must be carefully worded to avoid leading users to the answer.

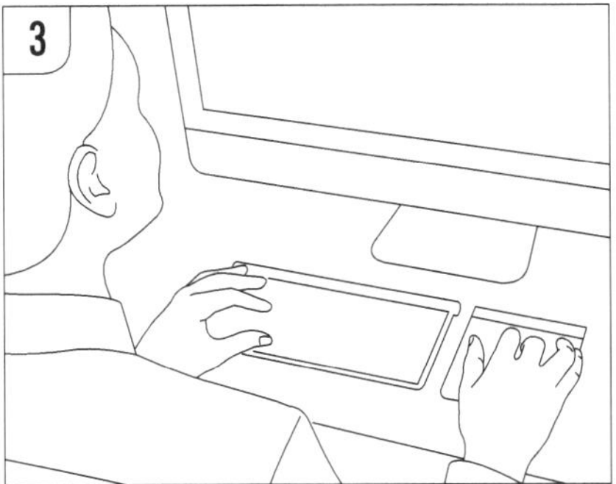

Test the Prototype: The design is placed in front of a user. Using the prepared task statement from step 2 have the user complete the task.

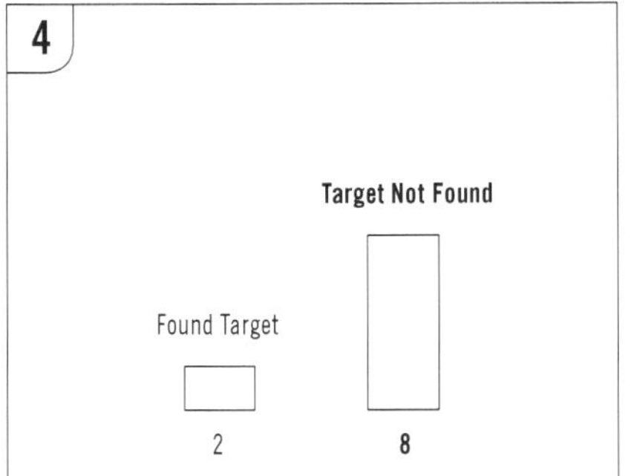

Repeat as Needed: The team repeats the test on 10 users. The first few users successfully found the correct target, but the last 8 users got it wrong.

Rinse and Repeat: Users were not able to consistently select the correct region of the design so the team alters the prototype and repeats the test on new users.

Method Reference: https://www.usability.gov/how-to-and-tools/methods/first-click-testing.html

Five Second Test

In a five second test you show the user a design for five seconds and then ask some follow-up questions to discover their first impressions.

To conduct a five second test simply put the design in front of the user for 5 seconds and then take it away. Follow this with a set of questions about the design. Repeat this on 5 or more users to understand how the design is performing. This can be automated with an online tool or you can use printouts of the design.

Sample follow-up questions:
- What products or services are being provided?
- Who is the company?
- Is the brand trustworthy?
- What benefit does this product offer to the user?
- How does this product work?
- What does this product do?

While it is most common to give the users only 5 seconds, the number is not set in stone. In some cases you might want to give users as much as 60 seconds, to review a page. For example you might use 60 seconds to test if users develop a deeper understanding of a complex topic after reviewing a long web page.

When to use: When you need to understand a user's first impression or what stands out to them.

Difficulty: Easy   **Time:** 1 Hour   **Participants:** 5+

Five Second Test Example

A new feature product on a homepage is being explored. The impact on the user's first impression needs to be known. This method works well because it is quick to use and encourages participants to share their first thoughts.

Prepare Questions: Write a set of simple follow-up questions. Here the goal is to discover what the user recalls about the new featured area.

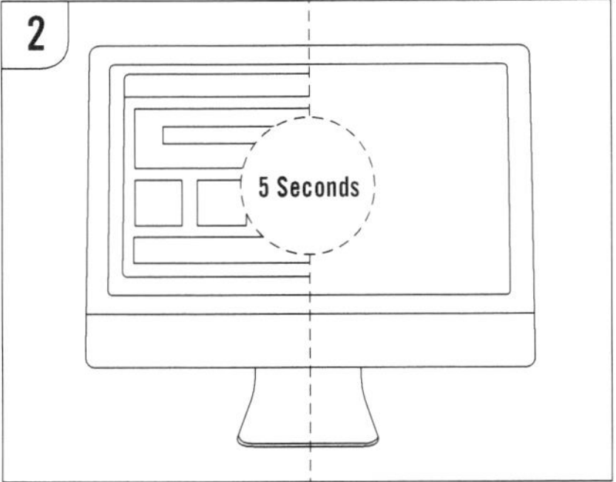

Start 5 Second Test: Allow the participant to see the design for 5 seconds.

Answer Questions: Have the participant answer the follow-up questions.

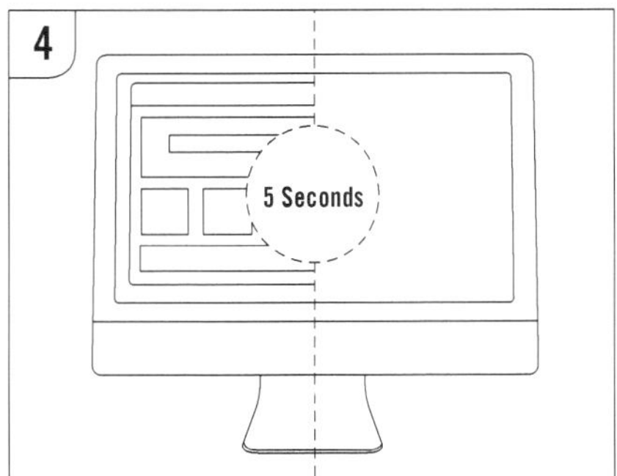

Repeat: Repeat on at least five other participants in order to get a balanced set of results.

Process Results: In the results look for answers that match the desired goal. You know you're done iterating when the majority of the participants answer the way you hoped they would. In this case it might be that they felt positive about the new feature area.

Five Whys Analysis

Five whys is a series of "why" questions that are used to find the root cause of a person's behavior and motivation.

Start by asking a broad question about the user's behavior based on the given problem. After they answer the question, follow it up with the question "Why?" Do this five times, documenting any key motivations that are revealed along the way. Try to avoid horizontal or leading questions that don't move the conversation towards the root cause.

One of the benefits of the five whys analysis method is that it gets the other person talking. It can help you dig past the surface answer and discover a deeper meaning behind a user's behavior or thoughts. It also prevents you, the researcher, from speaking your opinion and altering how the participant might otherwise respond.

When to use: During an interview or conversation in order to dig for details.

Difficulty: Very Easy   **Time:** 30 Minutes   **Participants:** 5+

Five Whys Analysis Example

A restaurant has a new digital menu/payment system. The team wants to learn why customers are not using the digital payment feature and still paying the traditional way with the server. This method works to determine the root cause by pealing back the layers of confusion.

Ask Broad Opening Question: As the user leaves the restaurant, ask the user, "Did you use the new digital menu system to pay your bill?"

They answer, "No":

Why? I didn't see anyone else using it, so I didn't try either. (First why)

Why? Because I didn't want to be the first to try it. (Second why)

Why? I go out to eat to relax and don't want to figure something new out. (Third why)

Why? I don't think I am good with new technology. (Fourth why)

Why? Because it's not something I use in my daily life. (Fifth why)

Ask Five Whys: Follow up the opening question with five why questions to peel back the layers and get to the core of the problem.

Interpret The Results: After the five whys you see the core problem wasn't the fact that others weren't using it, but rather the lack of familiarity with the type of interface.

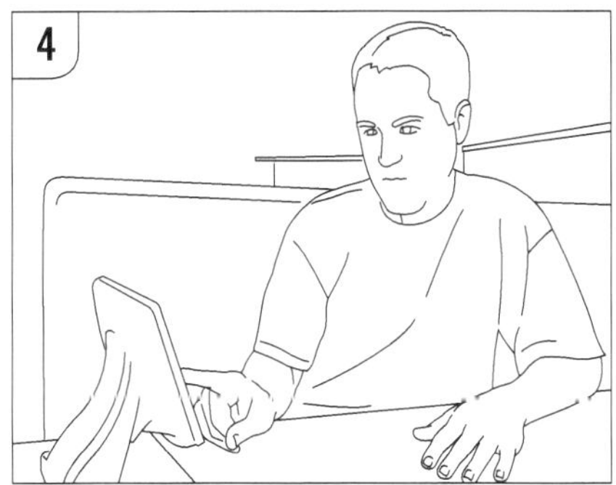

Repeat: The researcher repeats the test with many customers in order to build a collection of reasons why customers either use or bypass the new system.

Freelisting

Freelisting is when a person is asked to list as much information as possible in order to gain a better understand of a user's mental model.

On a large piece of paper write the question at the top. State the question such as "Would you please list all the _________ that you _________?" Communicate to the participant how long they have and not to worry about their handwriting. A good place to start is to give each participant 10 minutes. To help understand the results, group the responses into categories and look for common themes.

Here are some examples of freelisting questions:
"Would you please list all the situations in which you use this app?"
"Would you please list all the functions that you use in the program?"
"Would you please list all the limitations you saw in the app?"

While it might seem very similar to brainstorming, freelisting is used for gathering data where brainstorming can be more focused on creative ideation. Also, in freelisting, participants can answer in any way they like, while a survey has a fixed set of responses to pick from.

When to use: When you want to discover what users associate with your product.

Difficulty: Average   **Time:** 4 Hours   **Participants:** 5+

Freelisting Example

A software team working on a to-do list tool is looking to expand the core features. The team needs to know more about how often and where customers are using the product. Freelisting is perfect for collecting this information since customers can recall these types of details.

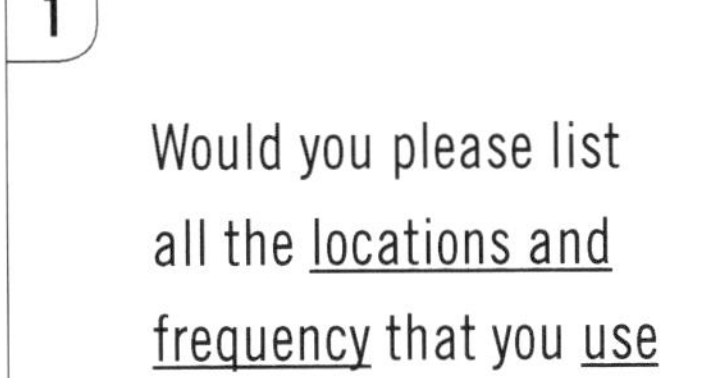

Define the Question: Using the question template (on page 48) the team forms the research question.

Collect Data: One participant is asked to spend 10 minutes answering the question with as many answers as possible.

Repeat the Test: The team repeats the test until they have results from 5 participants.

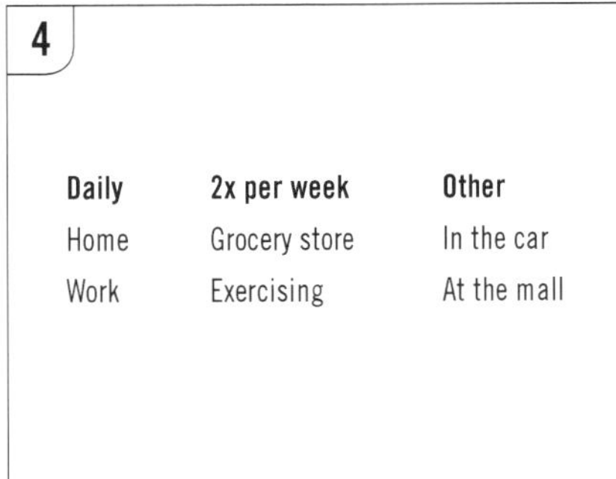

Organize the Results: The responses are gathered together and grouped into common categories. The frequency of each task is also indicated.

Consider Next Steps: The team has a much better idea of where their application is being used. Now they are able to explore ideas and prototypes to improve the system.

Future Workshop

A future workshop allows stakeholders to work together to create a vision for a product or an experience years into the future.

Before starting a future workshop you must identify the product or feature set you are going to be casting a vision for. Once you have a target in mind you can step through the four phases of the method:

1. Preparatory Phase: Prepare for the workshop by collecting existing research, establishing rules for the workshop, and scheduling the event.

2. Critique Phase: The stakeholders work together to examine the current experiences to better understand the current state.

3. Fantasy Phase: In this step participants communicate their unrestricted dreams and visions. The team navigates these and identifies an agreed-upon set of goals.

4. Implementation Phase: Create a feasible plan to implement elements from the vision into the product. This step takes the radical thinking from step 3 and puts it into more practical steps that can be achieved.

When to use: When you need to establish a future vision to work towards.

Difficulty: Very Hard   **Time:** 4 Hours   **Participants:** 20+

Future Workshop Example

A software development team is planning to rebuild an inventory management application for an automated network of warehouses and distribution centers. The team has conflicting ideas for the primary goals of the rebuild. They use this method because it allows everyone to express their ideas in a structured way that pushes the team to a single common vision.

Preparatory Phase: The team leader plans the structure of the workshop. The team is asked to research the competition and sketch ideas ahead of time.

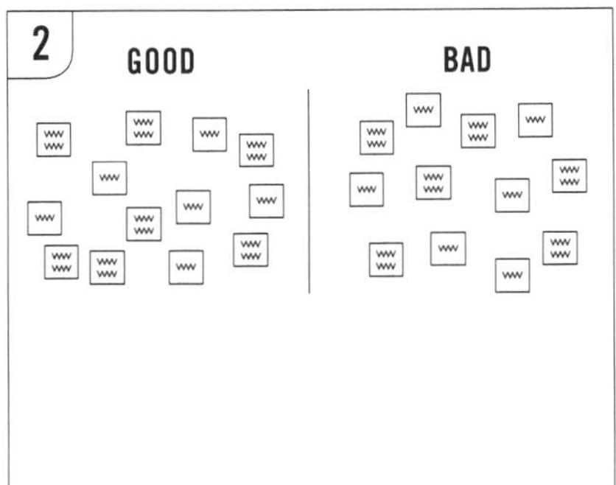

Critique Phase: Using Post-it notes the team notes all of the good and bad elements of the current system. These are sorted into groups.

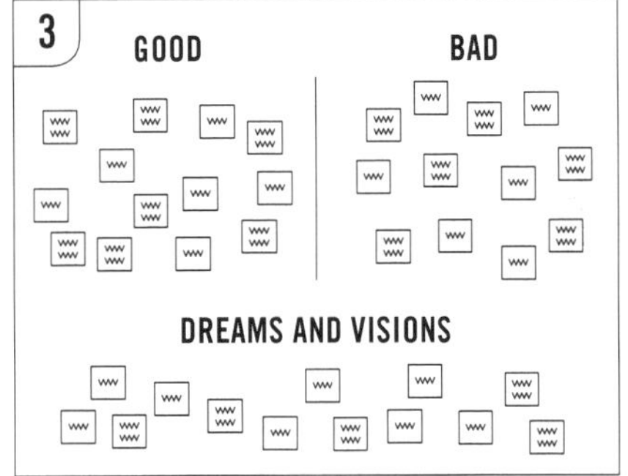

Fantasy Phase: The team adds to the collection of notes by brainstorming ideas about what they would hope for in the new version of the software.

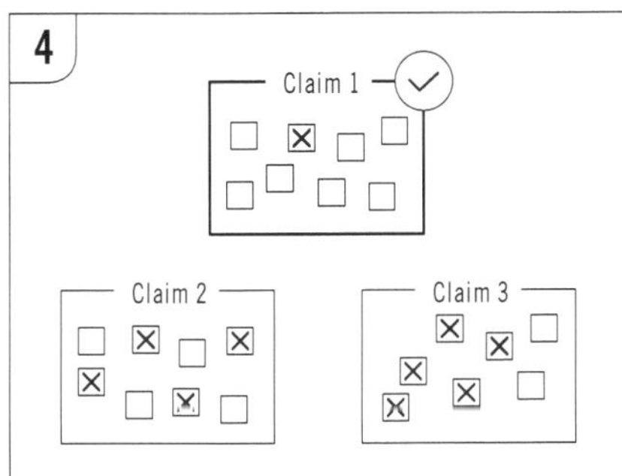

Implementation Phase: The team decides to use another method, like the Claims Analysis method on page 20, to assess each of the ideas and strategize what will be included.

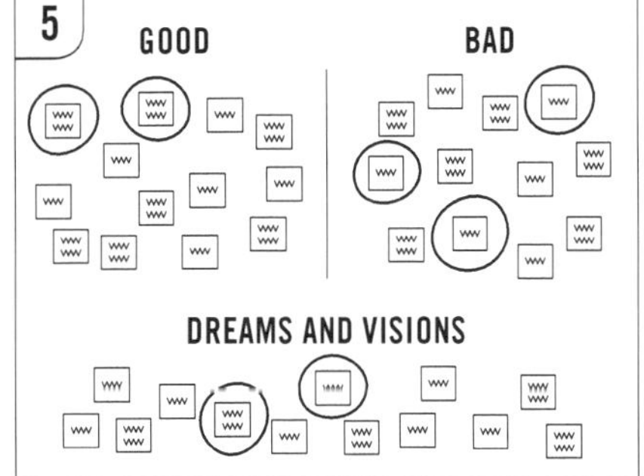

Create a Common Vision: The team is able to clearly see bad elements to avoid, good elements to carry forward and new ideas to introduce. This helps them move forward with a common vision.

Method Reference: http://dux.typepad.com/dux/2011/02/method-6-of-100-future-workshop.html

Guerrilla Usability Testing

Guerrilla usability testing is based on impromptu user tests with the goal of quickly finding and fixing problems.

With guerrilla usability testing there is no need to plan a script or complex set of tasks ahead of time. All you need is to know what feature you're trying to test out. Step one is to find a test user; typically you want someone that does not have prior knowledge of the product. Ask the user to perform a few tasks related to the features you're interested in improving. Observe their behavior and note any problems you see them encounter. Finish this off by asking them about the experience. This should be a quick 15-minute interaction and should highlight details you need to continue to refine. A common approach is to do several guerrilla-style tests in quick succession.

This is often referred to as guerrilla testing because it is frequently done in public or urban settings like a coffee shop where you will have easy access to a stream of people. The biggest key in picking a location is to select one that will likely have people from your target user group.

When to use: When you have the flexibility to incrementally improve the product you're working on.

Difficulty: Average **Time:** 1 Hour **Participants:** 1+

Guerrilla Usability Testing Example

A researcher is creating a prototype for a new mobile application. She wants to make sure that users will understand the flow of the interface and she would like to quickly iterate on the design. Guerrilla usability testing will help her gather informal feedback and rapidly improve her design.

Choose a Location: Using her laptop she to work in a common area where she will have access to many people, like a coffee shop, library or park.

Start Quick Tests: As she works on her prototype she asks someone to try it out.

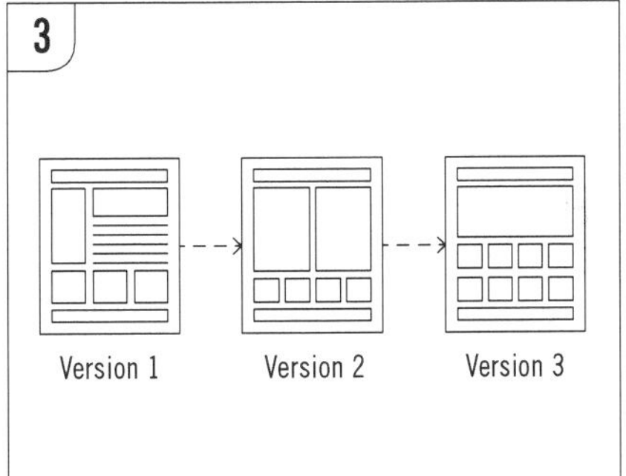

Iterate the Design: Based on the observation and feedback she identifies ways to refine the prototype.

Repeat the Test and Iteration: She continues doing this for the whole day and has tested the designs with about 12 different people when she is done.

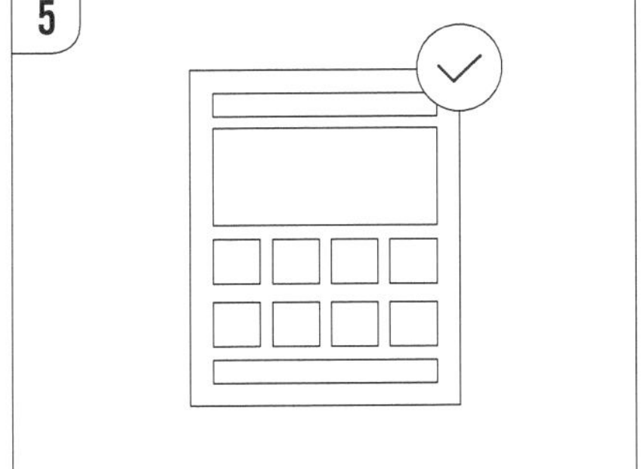

Review Results: At the end of the day she has a well-refined prototype that incorporates a lot of user feedback.

Heuristic Evaluation

The heuristic evaluation uses a predefined list of guidelines and is conducted by a UX expert.

A UX expert uses the following guidelines to review the system:

1. Visibility of system status: The user should always be aware of what is happening with the system through feedback and messaging.

2. Match between the system and real world: The system should use language expected by the user and follow any real-world patterns for the type of scenario.

3. User control and freedom: The system should allow users to work in multiple ways and to undo incorrect choices.

4. Consistency: The system should use the same language, visual styles and similarly structured workflows whenever possible.

5. Error prevention: The system should help the user avoid errors.

6. Recognition over recall: The system should minimize what the user has to remember or memorize and instead help them recall things through visual elements.

7. Flexibility and efficiency: Users should be able to move through the system in various ways depending on their skill level.

8. Aesthetics: The visuals should not interfere with the system.

9. Recovery from errors: Error messages are easy to understand.

10. Help and documentation: The system should provide access to documentation that guides users through common tasks.

When to use: Use as an initial method to proactively address usability issues.

Difficulty: Hard   **Time:** 2 Days   **Participants:** 0

Heuristic Evaluation Example

An outside UX researcher has been asked to evaluate a software product's usability. A heuristic evaluation is a great solution because it provides a structured format for assessing the product's usability. Also, the method does not rely on users and can therefore happen very quickly.

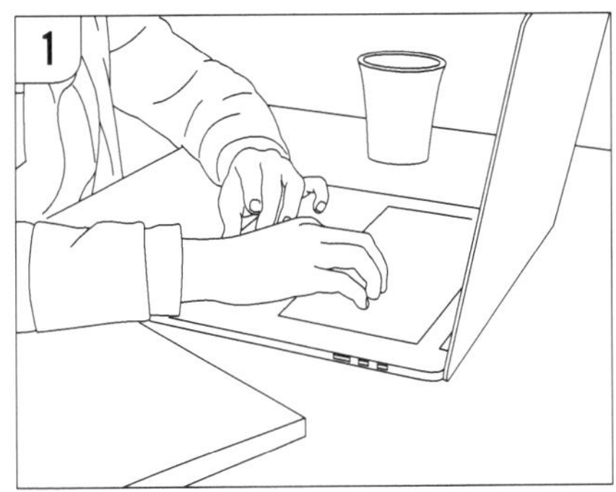

Know the Product: Before the researcher can assess the product she spends a few hours learning how the application works and what the primary functions are.

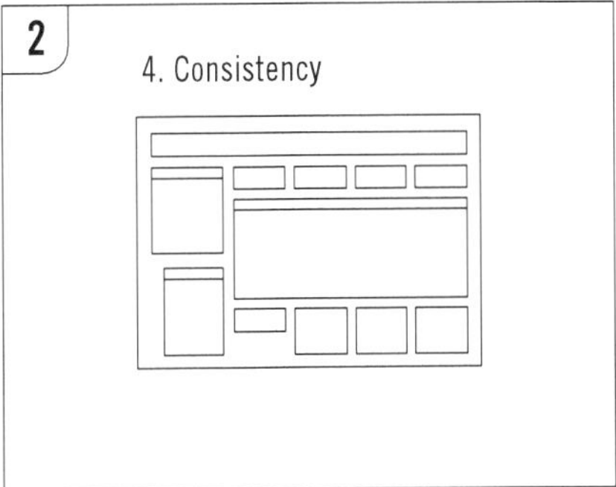

Get Set Up: Set up a document with a section for each of the heuristics (listed on page 54).

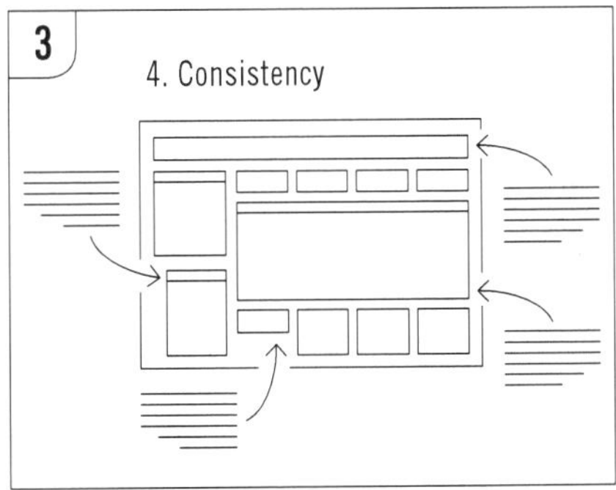

Analyze the System: Step through each of the heuristics and assess the system in relation to each one. Include screenshots to best capture the results.

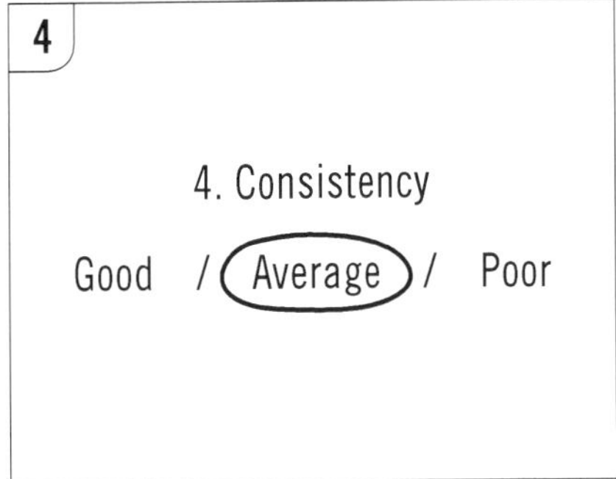

Summarize: One helpful technique is to score the system on each of the 10 heuristics. This can serve as an executive summary at the beginning of the report.

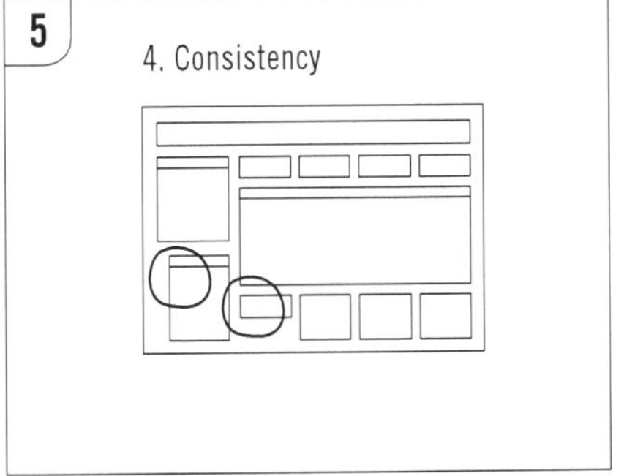

Inform the Team: With this assessment the team can begin to address the areas with the most usability problems.

Hot Air Balloon

The hot air balloon method is a visualization that helps teams compare and group the constraints and advantages of a product or an experience.

Start by drawing a large hot air balloon on a whiteboard. Using Post-it notes identify negative elements or aspects that will hold the balloon down; these are elements holding the project back. Then, do the same thing for the positive elements or aspects and place them in the balloon; these are the elements that would make the project a success. After all the Post-it notes are placed, the team can group similar topics and themes. Discuss the groupings and their key factors, and then form a plan of action based on the results of the discussion.

The visualization helps the team get a full view of the various options and the pros/cons of each. This is often a helpful method for cutting through a team's assumptions or biases towards certain approaches.

When to use: It can be done as a major starting point for a product or an experience.

Difficulty: Easy	**Time:** 1 Hour	**Participants:** 5+

Hot Air Balloon Example

A chain of retail stores is considering how it might use technology to enhance the customer experience in order to increase sales. The team needs to assess their many ideas; each of which has significant barriers. The hot air balloon method will help them quickly visualize the strengths and barriers for each of their ideas.

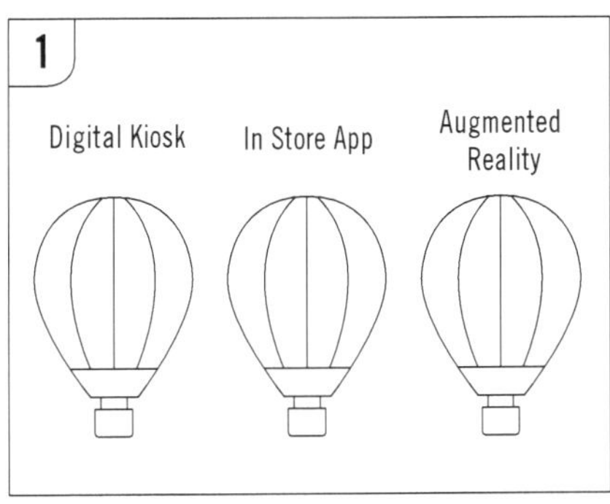

Draw the Balloons: To begin the team uses a whiteboard to draw 3 large hot air balloons. Each of which will be used to assess a single major idea.

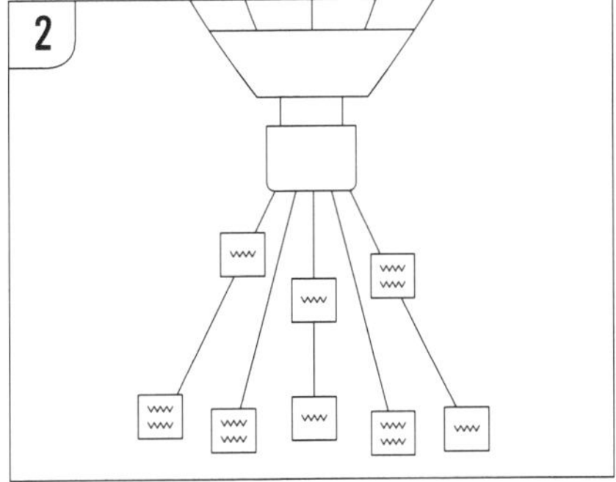

Add Negative Elements: The team adds Post-it notes below each balloon for all of the negative aspects that will hold the idea back. Ex. Digital Kiosk: expense, floor space, stationary, etc.

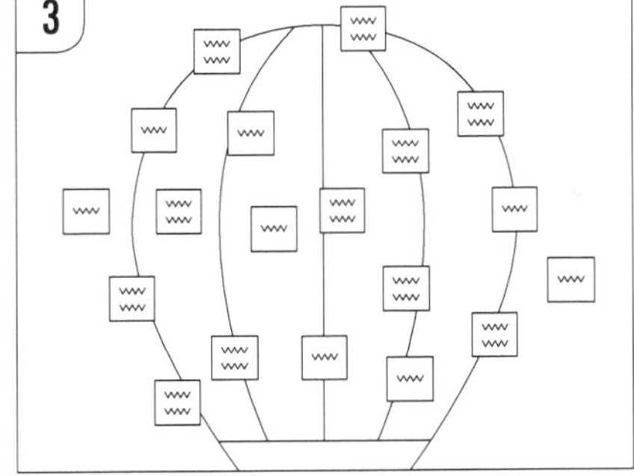

Add Positive Elements: Next, the team adds Post-it notes inside the balloon for each of the positive aspects of the idea. Ex. Digital Kiosk: many functions, location awareness, no download needed, etc.

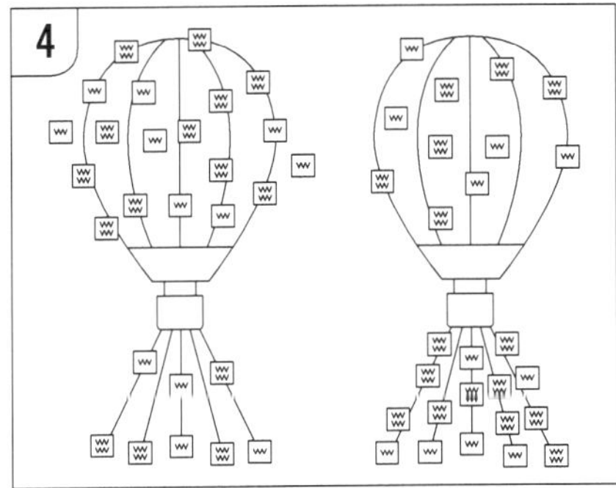

Look for Patterns: The team can now see how the various ideas compare. They quickly eliminate one idea due to obstacles that outweigh the benefits.

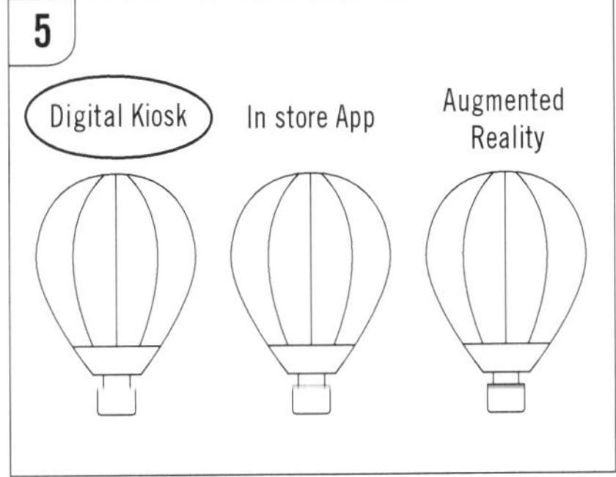

Move Forward: With this fresh perspective the team is able to select an idea to pursue that has a good balance of negative and positive elements.

I Like, I Wish, What If

I Like, I Wish, What If (IL/IW/WI) is a question-based framework to gain constructive feedback from a group.

First, it helps to designate someone as an information recorder; this will allow the conversation to flow between the participants. As a group discuss a topic by starting sentences with either I Like, I Wish or What If. Each group member should listen to each person's statement, but does not have to respond to each one. IL/IW/WI framework helps encourage team members to provide feedback that is clear and expresses their point of view.

Here are some sample responses:
"I like when we had mid-progress meetings."
"I wish we hand more time to visit with the client in person."
"What if we explored new UX methods at the start of the project?"

This method can be used with internal team members, clients or even a group of users. The structured format encourages participants to speak up and spark conversations.

When to use: When you need a direct way to increase constructive feedback between team members.

Difficulty: Easy　　　　　　**Time:** 1 Hour　　　　　　**Participants:** 2+

I Like, I Wish, What If Example

An existing museum exhibition is being updated, and new digital technology is being considered. They want to explore what aspects of the current exhibition to keep and what new aspects to add on. The team decides to use I like, I wish, what if because it addresses both current positive aspects and other possibilities not thought of.

Gather Stakeholders: The external creative team and museum employees gather together.

Designate Recorder: Have one person take notes for the group.

Allow Participant Statements: Allow each participant to state an "I Like, I Wish and What If" statement without interruption from others.

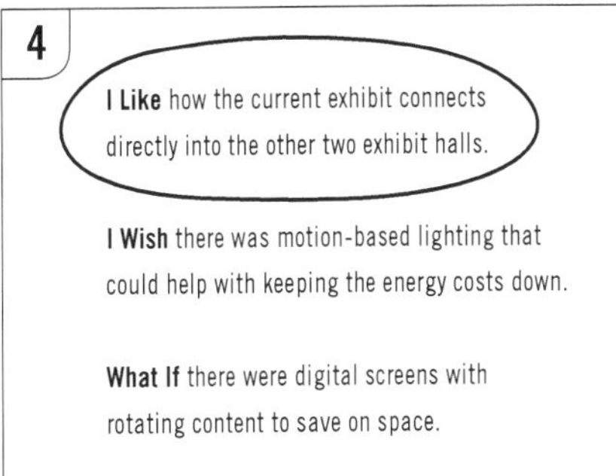

Review Results: As a group review and discuss each statement. Decide which ones are worth exploring further.

Conduct Additional Research: Based on the results, here the team can conduct further research to determine the value of each idea.

Icon Usability Test

Use an icon usability test to discover the meanings users associate with an icon.

There are two primary ways to test user's interpretation of an icon:

The first approach is to test how users interpret the icons in isolation. Show the users one icon at a time and ask them to list up to five keywords they would associate with the icon. If you need to test multiple options for a single icon, it is recommended to test each option on a different set of users. This provides insight into the raw meaning the icons have without the bias of your full interface. This is a great way to ensure that the icons you select reflect a useful message even without the rest of the interface.

The second approach is to show users the full interface with the icons in place. Have the user describe the functionality or information each icon will allow access to. This approach helps to discover if the icons reflect an accurate message within the context of the full design. It is common to start with the first approach when selecting icons and follow it up later with the second to ensure that the icons are working well.

When to use: When connecting icons to a meaning for the first time or when using less common icons.

Difficulty: Average   **Time:** 4 Hours   **Participants:** 5+

Icon Usability Test Example

A healthcare company is building a tool to allow users to chat with a doctor in real time. They need an icon to represent this functionality but there is not an industry standard. They want to make sure users correctly interpret the meaning of the icon. An icon usability test will help them discover what users associate with each icon they have selected.

Collect the Icons: Begin by collecting the various versions of the icon the team wants to try out.

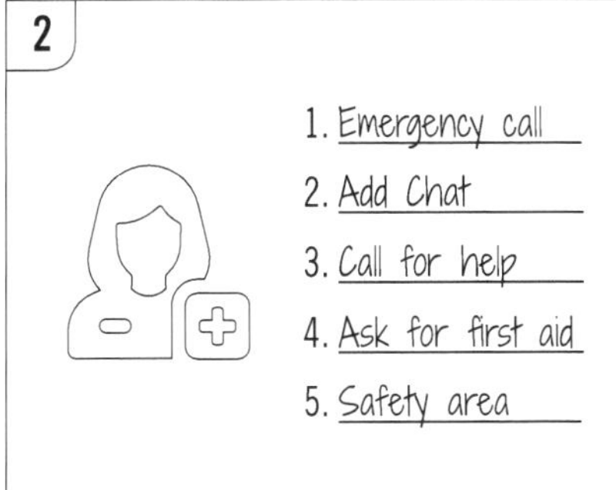

Test the Icons: Show each potential user only one icon. Ask them to list 5 keywords they would associate with it.

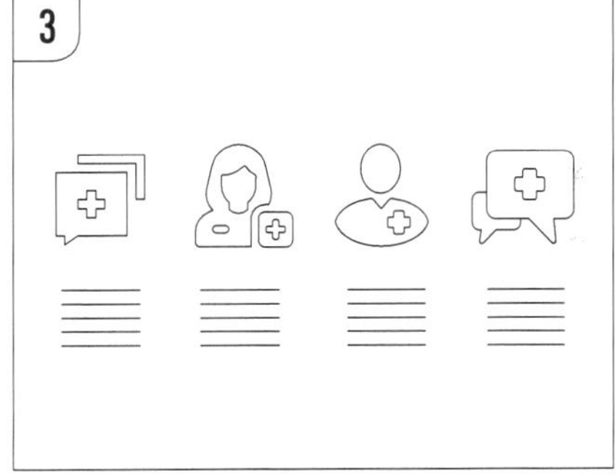

Repeat the Test: Continue testing until each icon has been tested on 5 or more different people.

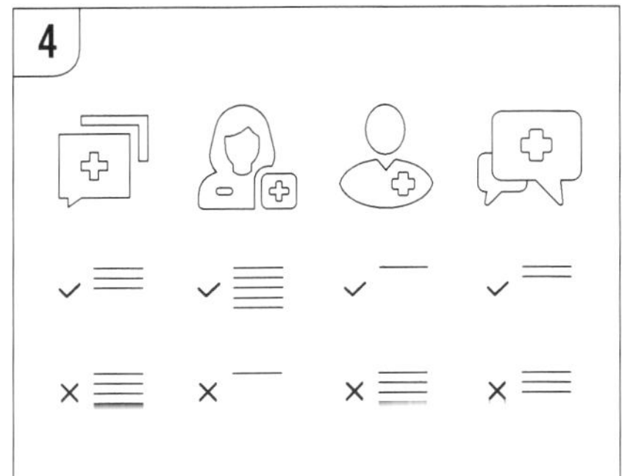

Collect the Results: All of the keywords for each icon are collected together and grouped based on how close they are to the intended meaning.

Select the Icon: Based on the results the team is able to select the icon that users most consistently associate with the desired meaning.

Informal Usability Testing

With informal usability testing researchers observe participants completing an assigned task to identify ways it might be improved.

The first step is to define the tasks you are going to have users perform. Prepare any assets that will be needed by the user (such as a prototype). Prepare a simple script or outline to use while directing the user through the study.

The next step is to run the test one participant at a time. Ask the user to complete the tasks and observe them as they work. Take notes on their behaviors, points out where they hesitate or take wrong steps, and anything of interest in their work.

After running the test on 5 or more participants create a list summarizing your findings. Put the most common elements at the top. The list contains the pain points you would like to refine. Research shows that testing with 5 participants will reveal 80 percent of the problems. More tests start to reveal the same problems.

This method differs from guerilla testing (page 52) in that a guerilla test has no preparation at all; you just quickly have a user try out your system. In contrast informal usability testing has more structure and runs the same test on multiple users.

When to use: Before, during or after the development of a feature begins.

Difficulty: Average   **Time:** 4 Hours   **Participants:** 5+

Informal Usability Testing Example

Based on some requirements a new feature for a movie streaming service has been prototyped. While stakeholders have approved it, the team wants to make sure users will be able to easily use it. The team needs to identify any major usability issues. An informal usability test will help them discover where users might have problems using the system.

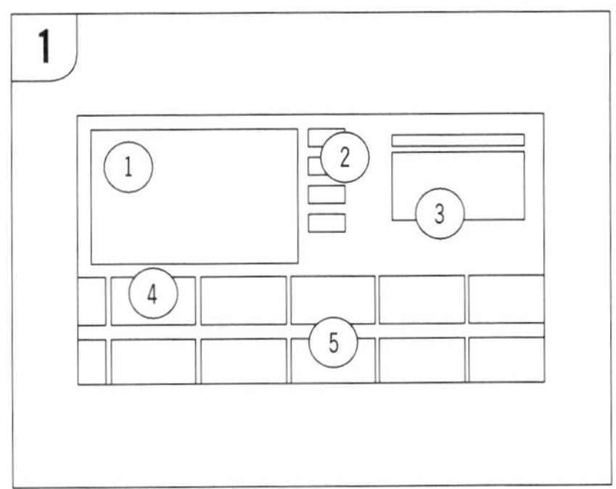

Define the Tasks: To begin, the team identifies the key tasks they want to test.

Plan the Study: A simple script is prepared to ensure that each test is conducted in the same way.

Test Users: Using the script to direct each participant the team tests the prototype on 5 different users.

Take Notes: During each test the team takes notes based on the user's actions, questions and comments.

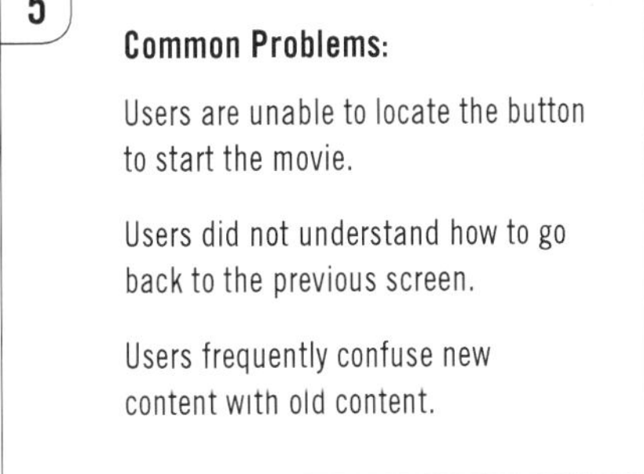

Interpret Results: Using the results the team is able to identify the most common usability problems users encountered.

Method Reference: https://www.nngroup.com/articles/why-you-only-need-to-test-with-5-users/

Interviewing Users

Interviews are a series of open-ended questions designed to give you insight into what the user is thinking or feeling.

First, you must decide when the interview is to be conducted. For example you can interview users prior to a usability test before the user is biased by your design. In contrast you could interview users after a usability test with follow-up questions.

Second, create a plan for your interview. Write out the questions you want to ask each participant and leave space to fill in their responses. Having consistent questions makes it easier to assess the results after multiple interviews. Be mindful of the order of your questions in order to avoid biasing the participants' responses.

Finally, conduct the interview using the established questions that were planned out. Feel free to deviate from the interview plan and ask additional follow-up questions as it is appropriate. This loose structure is one of the benefits of conducting an interview.

A great combination is to use interviews for discovery and surveys to validate the findings that are true of a larger population. Also, if you record your interviews, there are services that will transcribe them for you so you can search and code them later.

When to use: Before and after UX methods that directly involve users.

Difficulty: Average   **Time:** 1 Hour   **Participants:** 1+

Interviewing Users Example

A team wants to understand how families plan, shop and prepare meals. The research team has a limited amount of time and would like to collect a wide range of ideas. They decide to use a structured interview that will help them collect this information.

Write the Interview: To begin, they write the interview using open-ended questions that will encourage participants to talk about key topics.

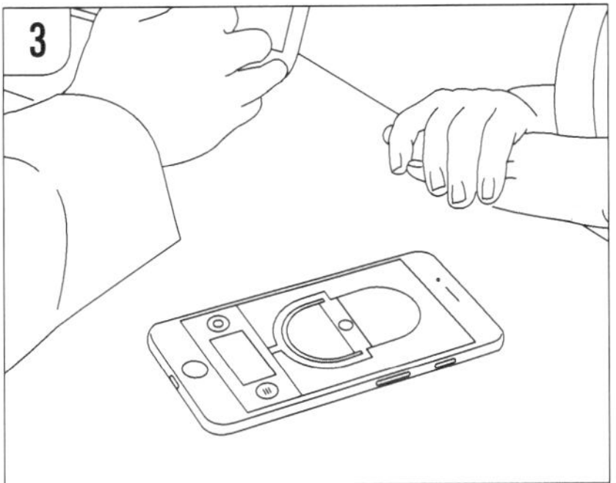

Conduct the Interview: The team wants a wide range of inputs and interviews 15 participants.

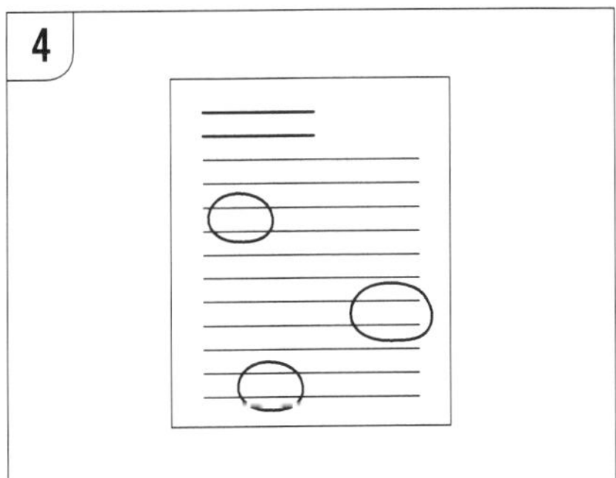

Take Notes and Record: During each interview the team takes notes about key points. They also record each session so they can refer back to it later.

Look for Patterns: The team analyzes the results to identify patterns and themes.

Report Findings: The team generates a summary document highlighting the key findings. This concise summary helps the team focus on the most important discoveries.

Journey Map

Journey maps are a visual timeline of a customer's experience as they work towards a goal.

Identify a user type you would like to profile in the journey map and go into the field to observe them. Your goal is to discover all the steps the user went through in order to achieve the given goal, what obstacles did they overcome and, most importantly, what was their emotional reaction at each step. Whenever possible you want to actually observe a user going through this; but in some cases you will simply have to ask them.

Once you have completed your user research it is time to build the visualization. A journey map typically includes these components:

The Setup: This section explains the scenario, the type of user and the goals that the user is trying to achieve.

The Experience: This section describes the stages the user goes through and their emotional experience at each step of the process.

Insights: This section summarizes what has been discovered at each stage. Typically, this is a summary of opportunities to improve.

The visualization is typically presented as a horizontal flow from start to finish with an indicator of the emotional experience at each step. Note that a journey map is not a flow chart and it is not intended to map out every possible experience a customer might have.

When to use: When you need to gain a full view of the customer's experience.

Difficulty: Very Hard   **Time:** 2 Days   **Participants:** 4+

Journey Map Example

A university is exploring ideas on how they might improve the experience for new students. They would like to discover what the experience is like for a student to go from looking for information about the school to the first day of class. A journey map will help them plot out all the stages of the students' experience and highlight the highs and lows along the way.

Identify Participants: The team contacts 4 incoming students that are willing to participate in the study.

Interview: The team interviews participants about how they learned about the school and the application process. They pay close attention to how the student felt at each stage.

Observe in Real Time: Team members observe students as they continue through the process of enrolling, visiting the campus and eventually attending their first classes.

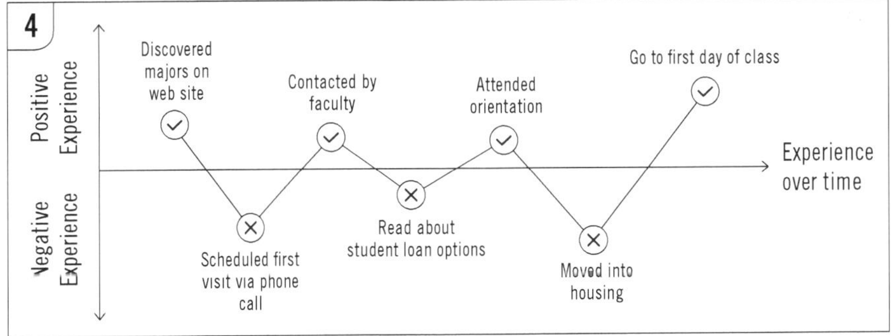

Plot the Results and Identify Problems: The entire experience for the participants is plotted out on a timeline. The vertical experience represents how positive or negative that step in the journey is. This visual artifact helps the university identify negative experiences they can work to improve.

Keyboard Level Modeling

Keyboard Level Modeling (KLM) estimates task time using predefined heuristics.

Identify a very small task you wish to analyze. Use the 5 heuristics below to estimate the time it will take to complete the task. Write a letter sequence using the letters to map out the steps to perform the task. Use as many of each heuristic as you need to represent the actual steps in the task. Then, add up the time in seconds. This is the estimated time it will take a user to complete the task.

KLM Heuristics:

K: 0.28 seconds for every **key** the user has to press.

P: 1.1 seconds to **point** the mouse at a target on the screen.

H: 0.4 seconds for the user to move their **hands** from the mouse to the keyboard and vice versa.

M: 1.35 seconds any time the user has to think or **make** a decision.

R: 0.75 seconds for the system to **respond** (load/update, etc.). Replace this time with an average response rate of the actual system.

KLM can be used to compare two versions of a task in order to estimate time savings. If version A takes 8.75 seconds and version B takes 7.25 seconds, you can estimate that version B will save about 1.5 seconds each time a user performs the task. This method is particularly useful in efficiency work on highly repetitive tasks.

When to use: When you need to maximize the efficiency of very small tasks.

Difficulty: Hard   **Time:** 4 Hours   **Participants:** 0

Keyboard Level Modeling Example

Software used to take customer orders over the phone in a pizza franchise is being revised. The team needs to reduce the amount of time it takes to enter orders so that call time can be reduced. The team has ideas for very small and detailed changes, but isn't sure if they will save time. Keyboard Level Modeling gives them a way to estimate task times to see if it might be an improvement.

1

Select the Task: The team identifies a task to streamline that is performed more than 1,000 times each day.

2

P - point at button

K - click the button

P - point at text field

K - click into the text field

H - move hands to keyboard

Kx5 - type 5 characters

P - point at submit button

K - click the button

= 6.34 Seconds

Model the Current Version: Using the heuristics on page 68, the task time for the current interface is estimated.

3

P - point at text field

K - click into the input field

H - move hands to keyboard

Kx5 - type 5 characters

Kx1 - press return to submit form

= 3.46 Seconds

Model the New Version: Using the same method, the time for the new version of the task is estimated.

4

The new version saves **2.88 seconds.**

Estimate Savings: The time for the new version is subtracted from the old version to see how much time is saved. Multiplied by 1,000 this is a savings of 48 minutes per day.

5

Estimated Savings

Task 1: 2.88 seconds

Task 2: 1.02 seconds

Task 3: 6.75 seconds

Conduct More Tests: The team repeats this process on many small tasks in the interface and identifies the most valuable changes to make.

Photojournal

A photojournal is a visual information-gathering method where the participant takes photos of their daily activities and everyday moments related to the research topic.

Over a multiple-day time span, have the participant take photos of their activities related to the subject matter that is being examined. For example, if research is being done on eating habits, have participants take photos of things like their meals, inside the refrigerator, grocery store shopping, dining, etc. Once enough photos are taken, send them to the person conducting the interview. Allow the interviewer time to examine the images and to create questions related to the photos.

When the interview takes place, ask the participant how they feel about the photos, why they took them and which ones did they leave out. By having the participant take photos ahead of time, they will have thoughts on the subject that will lead to a richer discussion of the topic at hand.

When to use: Before the interview stage, so questions can be formed.

Difficulty: Hard **Time:** 2 Days **Participants:** 1+

Photojournal Example

A health tool is being developed to help individuals manage their weight. The researchers want to learn the daily habits of the participants to aid in the planning of the tool. This method creates a visual reference and timeline that gives the researchers much needed insight.

1

Time period over 5 days.

Capture every meal and all ingredients.

Photo of the environment when you eat.

Photo of each plate of food before and after you eat it.

Determine Guidelines: Give the participants instructions on the topic being researched and encourage them to take as many photos as possible.

2

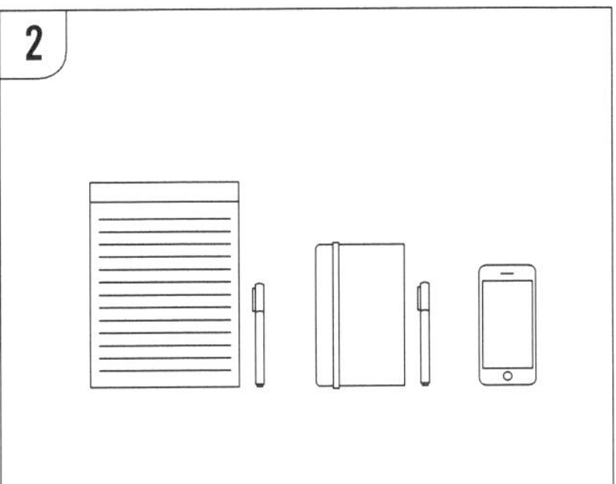

Supply Tools: Supply the participant with any tools needed to capture items for the photojournal. For this example, the participant will use a camera app on their own digital cell phone.

3

Capture Photos: Allow the participant a fixed amount of time to take photos of the activities being studied; typically 3-5 days depending on the topic.

4

Review Photojournal: Gather all the photojournal information and step through the photos with the participant. Through conversation attempt to understand what the user was thinking at each step.

5

Frequently eats in their car on the go.

Doesn't have a consistent nightly schedule to plan prepared dinners around.

Frequently meeting friends for meals.

Summarize Results: The researcher is now able to summarize the participant's daily habits that will aid in the planning of this new tool.

Pluralistic Walkthrough

A pluralistic walkthrough is when a group reviews an interface design all together at the same time to resolve usability issues faster.

Start by gathering the participants: a user, designers, developers, others not directly involved in the project, and a walkthrough coordinator. Place the design in front of the participants so they all can clearly see it. The coordinator then asks one question at a time. This is typically about a step towards completing a task. All the participants write down how they would complete the step. Allow the user to voice how they would work through the interaction first, and then the other participants can give their reasoning.

Once all the participants have shared their opinions, the coordinator reveals the correct or ideal choice. Make note of any changes that might need to happen. The coordinator will then share the next screen in the design and ask another question based on the task. Repeat this until all the desired questions have been answered.

The pluralistic walkthrough is very similar to the cognitive walkthrough. The key difference is that the pluralistic walkthrough is slightly less structured since it doesn't have the guiding questions. Depending on the scenario this can be helpful as it allows for more diverse conversations around the design.

When to use: When an early version of the design or prototype is ready to be tested.

Difficulty: Very Hard   **Time:** 4 Hours   **Participants:** 1+

Pluralistic Walkthrough Example

A team is attempting to refine a complex order fulfillment system that requires users to make use of multiple systems. The team is struggling to know how to make things easier to understand or where users might be confused. A pluralistic walkthrough will help by allowing the team to hear from multiple perspectives how participants would use the system.

1

Complete a customer order.

Add new customers to the system.

Look up order status.

Plan the Method: The researcher identifies the task that will be tested.

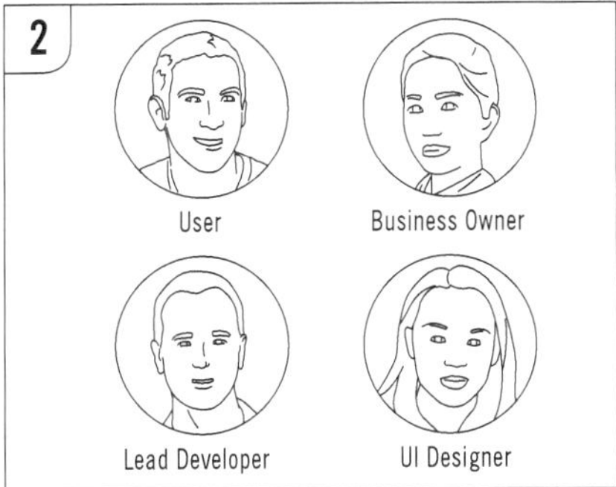

Gather the Participants: The team assembles the stakeholders, a user and several other people that are not directly involved in the project.

Go through Step by Step: The researcher asks the user "what is the first step you would take to complete the task?"

Discuss Each Step: For each step the user explains their choice. Then other team members ask questions and discuss the reasoning.

Repeat: The team repeats this until all the steps needed to complete the task are done.

Rapid User Profile

This is a process designed to rapidly create a detailed description of a user.

First, collect information about the user. To do this, interview a person that fits the demographics you wish to describe. The goal of the interview is to acquire the elements listed here:

- Ask about specific details about the person: physical traits, personal interests, a typical day in their life, etc.
- Ask them what thoughts and observations they have about the type of product you're researching.
- Observe and ask about emotional responses.
- Ask questions about how the product fits into their life.
- Look into any other details that relate to the user/product.

Use the interview results to write a profile. Use this list as a outline:

- Name the profile and include basic demographic data about the person you interviewed.
- Take a candid photo of the person (if they allow it) or a candid photo of any person fitting the demographic.
- Vividly describe the person in 1–3 paragraphs; help the reader create a mental image of this person.
- Use several paragraphs to describe the thoughts, observations, emotions and actions of the user as it relates to your product or your type of product.

When to use: When you need to help a team connect with and consider the user.

Difficulty: Average　　　　　　　**Time:** 4 Hours　　　　　　　**Participants:** 1+

Rapid User Profile Example

A team is interested in creating a line of kitchen utensils targeted at older people. The team is having trouble relating to the target audience. In order to build a long lasting perspective the team decides to write user profiles. The rapid user profile method helps them create these very quickly.

Interview a User: To begin, a team member interviews a user. She makes sure to ask questions as described on page 74.

Take Notes: The researcher makes sure to take lots of notes, including smaller details that will help her to write a believable profile.

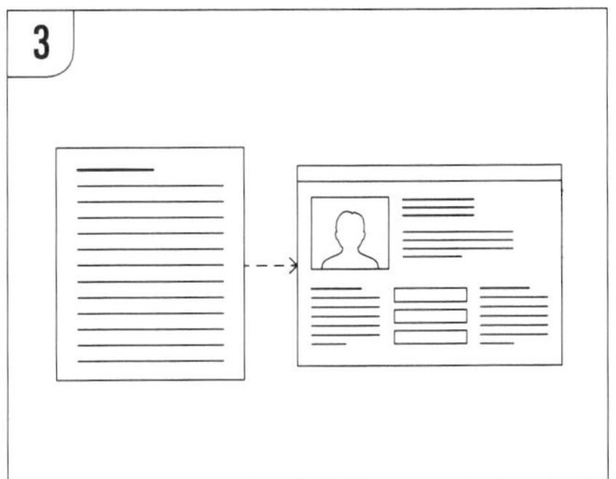

Write the Profile: Using the raw data the researcher writes a one-page user profile. She makes sure to include the sections outlined on page 74.

Repeat: The team interviews 2 additional users that represent different segments of their user base. A profile is created for each user.

Post the Profiles: The profiles are printed out and posted on the office walls. These profiles serve as reference points as the team works on the new products.

Real Time Conversational Feedback

Real time conversational feedback is when a participant sends short feedback messages while they take part in an experience in their own environment.

Send the participant the proper product or equipment to be tested. Determine the most natural way for the participant to send you a message, using any convenient messaging system. Text messages are a common solution that fit into most users' normal lives.

Allow the participant to interact with the product at their own convenience. While going through the experience they should send their reactions in conversational format to the researcher. If needed, follow-up questions to the feedback can be asked. The researcher can then take the feedback (reactions and feelings) and catalog it in the format of their choice.

This method creates a comfortable environment for the user to naturally use the product. This can lead to much more authentic and insightful feedback.

When to use: When a real life experience needs to be captured.

Difficulty: Easy   **Time:** 4 Hours   **Participants:** 5+

Real Time Conversational Feedback Example

A new board game is being designed and is ready for user playtesting. They want to learn how easily players can read and learn the rules. This method allows for real time feedback directly from the participant without any costly or complicated testing setup.

Determine Messaging Format: In this example the team decides to use SMS phone messaging because it won't interrupt the participants' experience.

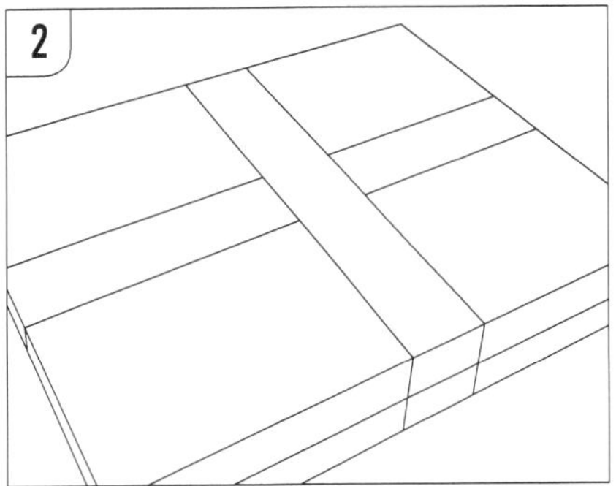

Send the Product: Send the game to the participant with instructions on how to provide feedback.

Receive Reactions during Experience: Have the participant send you feedback while learning and playing the game in their own environment.

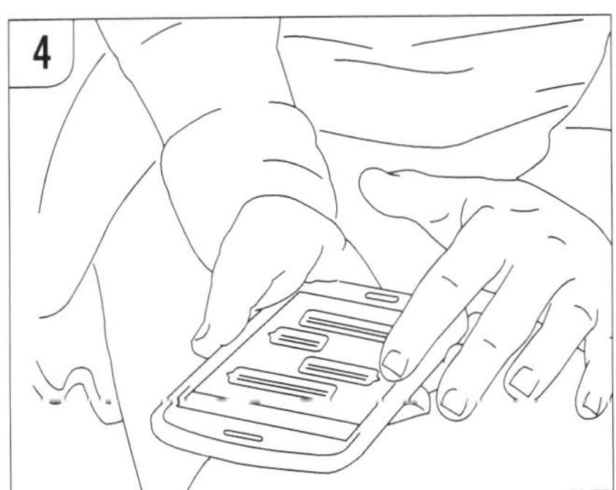

Ask Follow-up Questions: As the participant gives feedback, follow up with questions to gain more insight.

Catalog Findings: Record all the information gathered from the conversations and adjust the game as needed.

RITE Method

The RITE method (Rapid Iterative Testing and Evaluation) merges prototyping and usability testing into one process.

The RITE method begins with a prototype that is ready for testing on multiple users. After each user is tested, quickly decide if changes should be made to the prototype. Repeat this process of testing and refine as many times as you can. Sometimes a change is so obvious you can make it after observing a single user struggle with something. In other cases you will want to watch a few more users before deciding on changes.

The timeline for each test and refine cycle should be very quick. In a single day you should be able to do this on 4–10 users. In some cases teams will actually go where the application is being used and select participants in an ad hoc fashion.

When to use: When there is still a lot of flexibility in the feature being designed.

Difficulty: Average   **Time:** 4 Hours   **Participants:** 5+

RITE Method Example

In this example a team is working on a mobile navigation tool to be used by a driver in an automobile. The team wants to quickly iterate on the interface to eliminate major problems. The RITE method is a good fit for this task, as it provides a simple structure for rapidly improving a prototype based on direct user input.

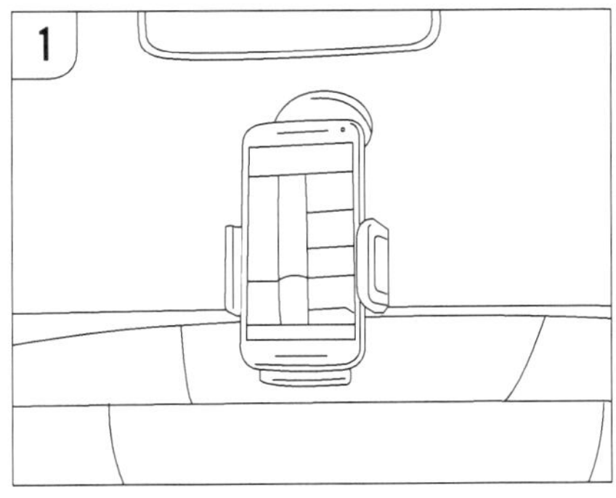

Set Up Test Environment: The team sets up the test environment including the prototype for the navigation tool.

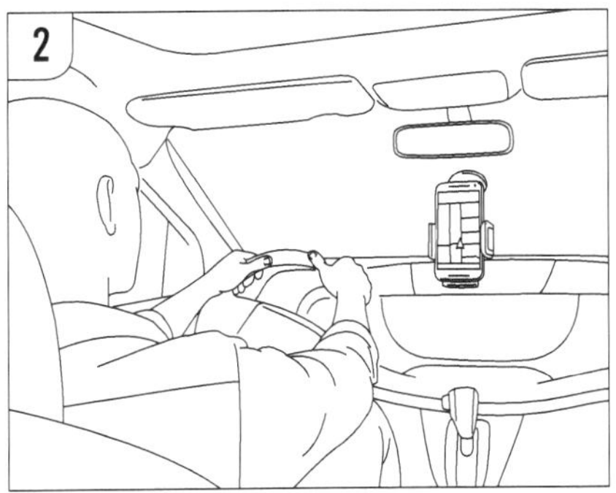

Test the Prototype: A single participant is brought in to test the system. The team observes and notes things to change.

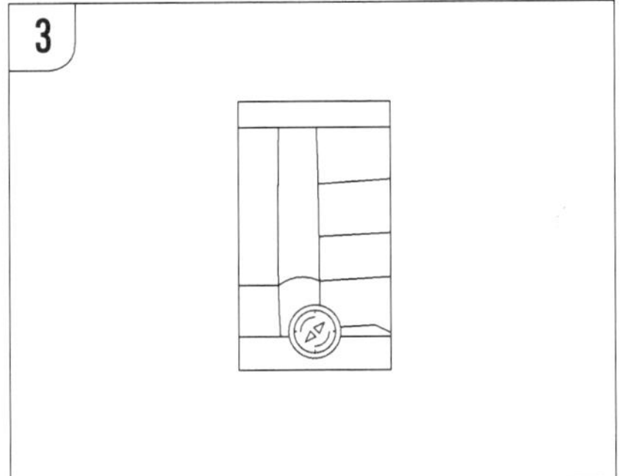

Refine the Prototype: The team quickly adjusts the prototype to eliminate pain points they observed before bringing in the next participant.

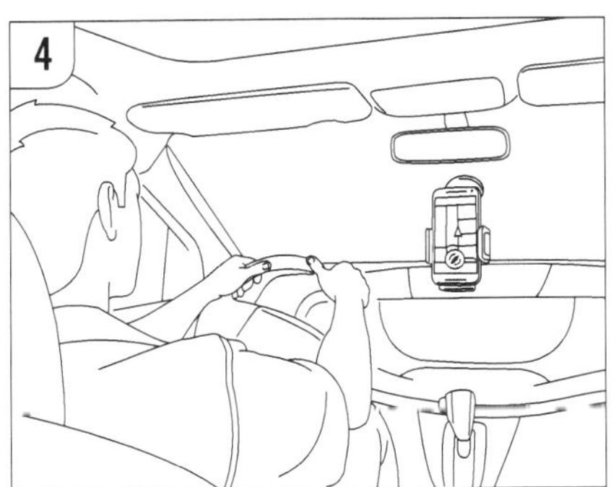

Repeat: Over the next 5 hours the team repeats this process on 8 more participants. Between each test they modify the prototype to eliminate problems.

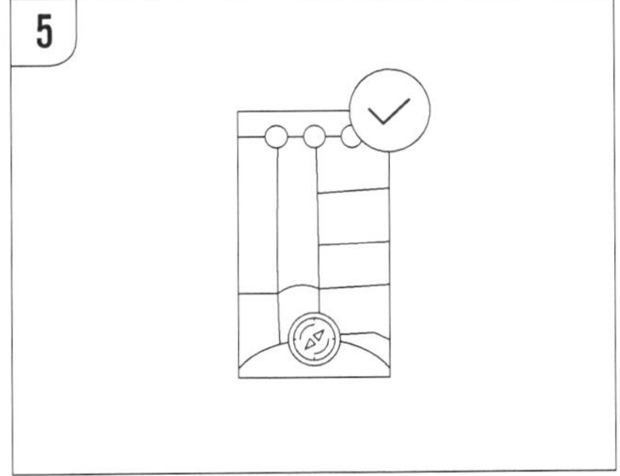

Finalize Results: At the end of the day the team has a much more refined prototype that has removed the most prominent pain points.

Semantic Differential Analysis

A semantic differential analysis measures emotional feedback (attitudes and feelings) by comparing bipolar adjective pairs on a scale.

Define 5 to 10 bipolar adjective pairs for your product or service and draw a line between each pair. These are word pairs that are opposite ends of a spectrum. For example, easy and hard or confusing and clear. When possible try to select words which relate back to either an attitude or a feeling the participant might have.

After having participants use a system or prototype have them complete the survey. For each word pair the user should indicate on the line how they feel best towards the system in relation to the two words. Do this with multiple users.

Finally, you can chart the results together. Collect all of the results and indicate them on a single chart. This way you can look for patterns or inconsistent responses. It can be very difficult to quantify user feelings. This is one way to attempt to do so.

When to use: When you need to quantify attitudes and feelings.

Difficulty: Very Hard　　　　**Time:** 4 Hours　　　　**Participants:** 5+

Semantic Differential
Analysis Example

A new time management utility is being tested. The team wants to learn the user's attitudes and feelings about it. This method works well because it provides an easy and consistent way for users to communicate their feelings.

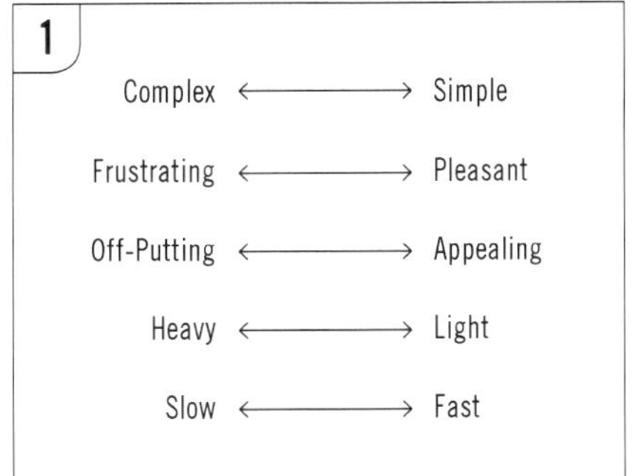

Create List: Create a list of bipolar adjective pairs.

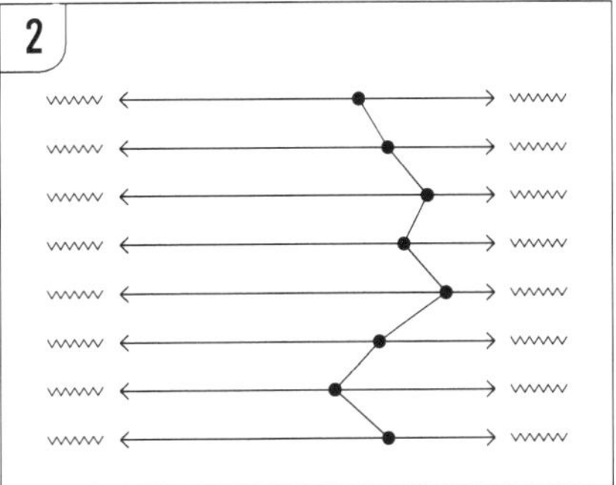

Survey User: Have a user mark the points on each line between the two adjectives that best represents their attitude towards the new utility.

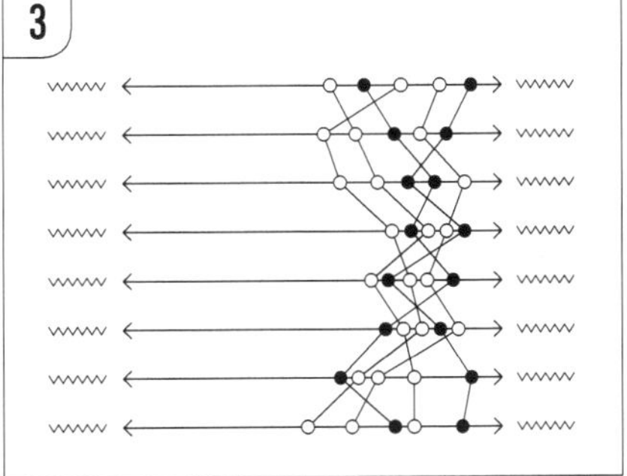

Survey Others: Survey at least four other users to reveal patterns of feelings.

Follow Up: The team assesses the results to see if users' feelings and attitudes align with the intended goals of the product.

Sentence Completion

A series of beginning sentences that are finished by a user based on a particular experience.

Start by creating the beginning of sentences with blank space at the end for the user to fill in. Depending on what information you need, the sentences can be open ended or more detailed. After the user has been through the experience, ask them each beginning sentence one at a time and allow them to finish it freely. They shouldn't over think it or take too long to finish the sentence as there is no right or wrong answer. There is no set number of sentences to be asked; ask as many as needed to address the questions based around the experience being explored.

Oftentimes, in the early stages of a design, it can be very difficult to know what pointed questions to ask. The open-ended nature of this method makes it a perfect solution when your design is still vague or in its early stages. By asking open-ended questions you can gather diverse thoughts and drive conversation more easily.

When to use: After a user has been through an experience.

Difficulty: Average   **Time:** 1 Hour   **Participants:** 5+

Sentence Completion Example

A digital key card system is being tested. It allows users to enter their hotel room, access a theme park and buy food all with one card. They want to learn what the users think of the experience with the new key card. This method allows for a quick reaction from the user and provides a structured format for the questioner.

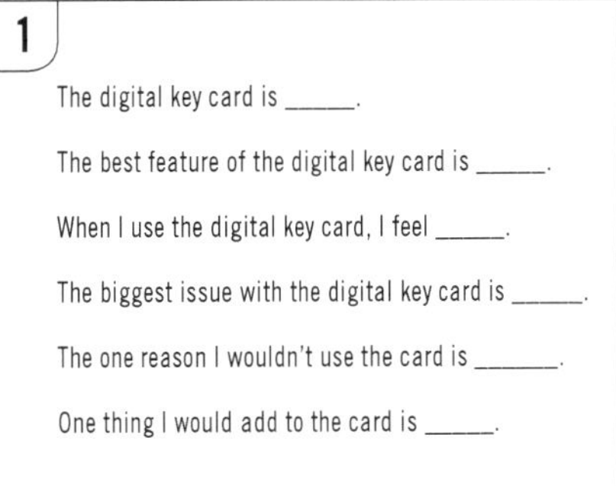

Prepare Beginning Sentences: Based on the participants' experience create beginning sentences related to what you want to learn about the system.

Use the System: Allow the participant to use the digital key card in all the different ways it can be used.

Finish Sentences: Allow participants to finish the sentences. Repeat the test with other participants.

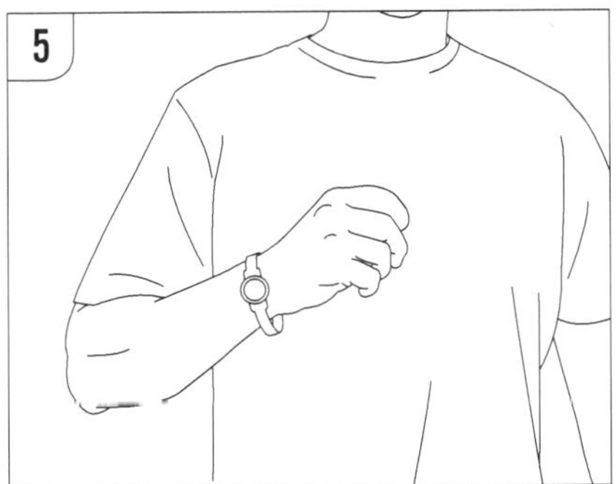

Identify Patterns: After reviewing the results the team notices that many users were worried about losing their cards.

Repeat with Changes: The team decides to repeat this method and test out alternatives that are more difficult to lose the card.

Single Ease Question (SEQ)

The single ease question is a 7-point scale for estimating how difficult a task is.

First, prepare the question and 7-point scale using a paper printout or digital tool. Format the question around this example: Overall, how difficult or easy did you find this task? Most often this exact version of the question works, but sometimes you must alter it slightly to have it make sense for the situation. The scale goes from 1 being "Very Difficult" to 7 being "Very Easy."

Next, have users complete the task you are researching. After users have completed the task have them answer the single ease question you prepared. If a users' rates the ease below a 5 it is recommended to immediately ask the user why they rated it this way. This can be incredibly helpful in identifying key usability problems. To get the ease rating, average the results.

A few ways this method can be used include:
- Follow up on a usability test to assess ease of use.
- To see how users rate a competitor's product to yours.
- To measure if changes to your product make it easier to use by comparing before and after scores.
- To compare the difficulty of two very different tasks.

When to use: When you need to quantify how easy something is to use.

Difficulty: Very Easy　　　　**Time:** 30 Minutes　　　　**Participants:** 1+

Single Ease Question Example

An email management system is being updated with a new organization feature. The team wants to learn if the updates are making tasks easier or more difficult. The single ease question method allows for quick insights and quantifiable data to review.

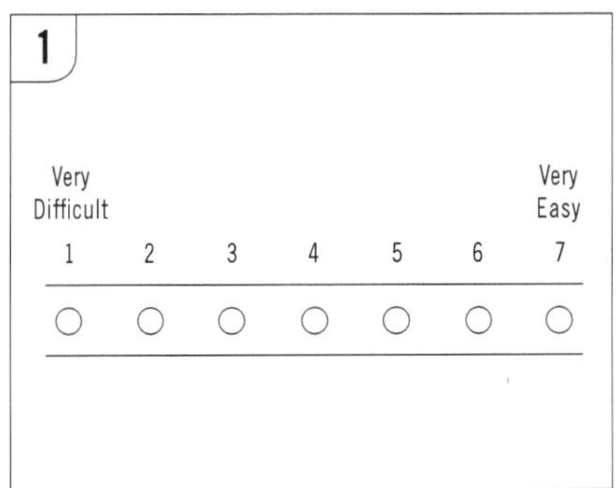

Set Up Scale: Create a 7-point scale going from very difficult at 1 to very easy at 7.

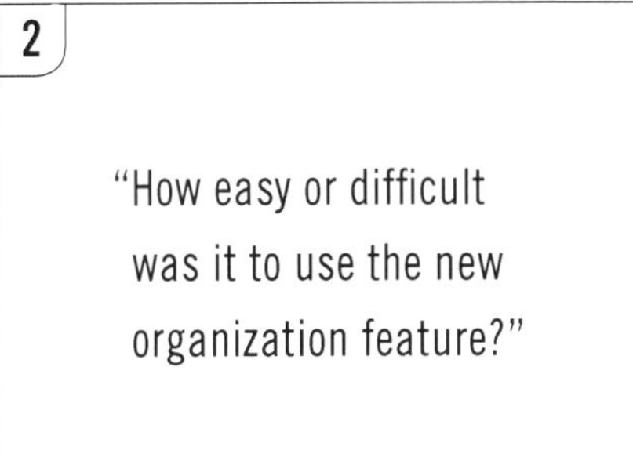

Write Question: Write the question based on the task being reviewed. In this case it's to see if the tasks involved with the email system update are easy to complete.

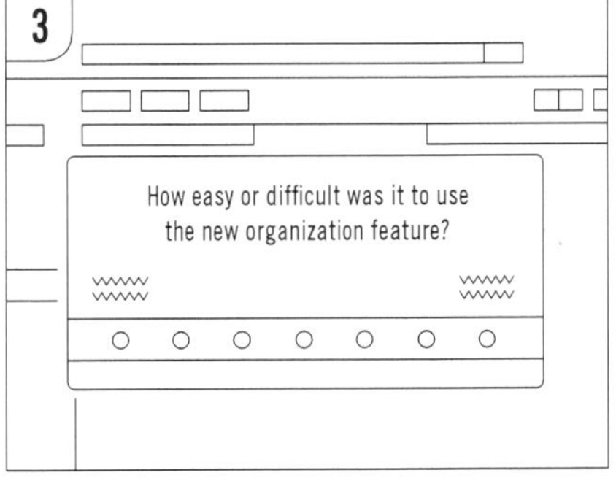

Place Question: Place the SEQ question and survey in a position where the user will see it right after the task, such as after a usability test.

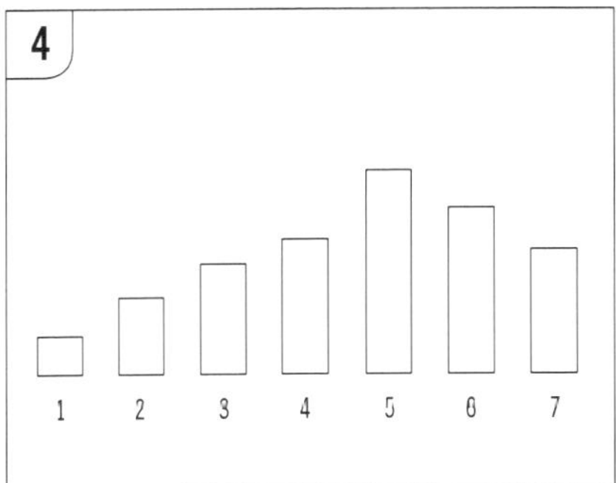

Compare Data: Compare the results of multiple surveys to determine the overall rating of the feature.

Static Evaluation and Markup

A static evaluation and markup is when users examine a static version of a user interface (UI) design, and are asked to explain what it does and mark it up with feedback.

Print out the UI design so that the evaluator has a free forming way to mark up the design. Ask the participant to explain the interface by writing on the design their thoughts on how the interface functions. Try to avoid explaining anything they are looking at or helping them out in any way. The user should try to note their interpretations of the interface as thoroughly as possible. One advantage of printing the design out is that the user cannot experiment with the interface to learn more; they are forced to provide feedback based only on what they see void of any function.

One approach is to have a group of people complete the task at the same time. This makes it a really fast method to use. If you do this, a great follow-up is to have a group discussion about the design.

When to use: Any time you need to make sure users correctly interpret UI elements.

Difficulty: Very Easy   **Time:** 1 Hour   **Participants:** 1+

Static Evaluation and Markup Example

Major UI changes to an employment web site are being made. They want to learn if the changes communicate the new features being added. This method makes sense because it forces users to communicate what they think something does without any additional information.

Prepare Evaluation: Print out the UI designs and supply markup tools like pens or markers.

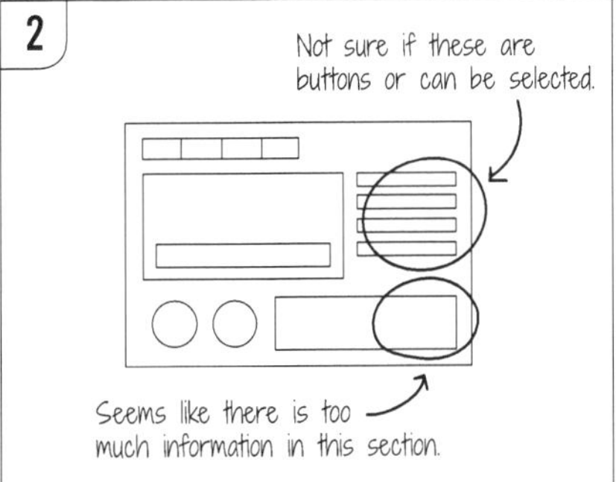

Mark Up: Have the participants mark up the UI design using visual and written annotations words, explaining what they think each element does.

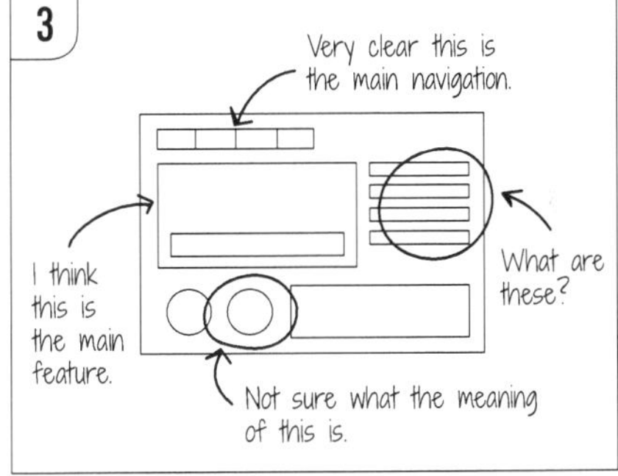

Repeat the Test: The team repeats the test on four additional users. This provides just enough data to recognize patterns in the way users interpret the design.

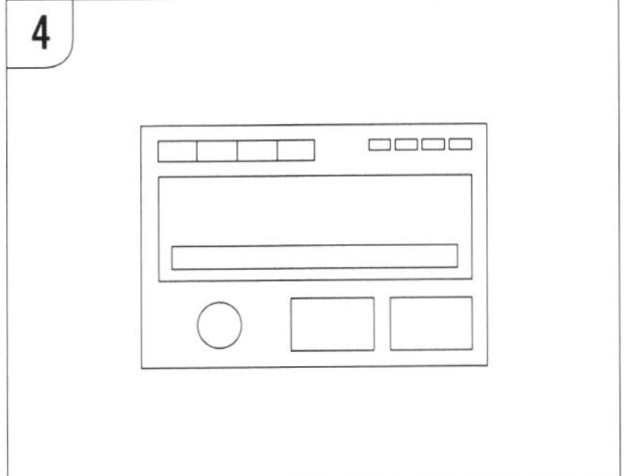

Revise the Design: Make adjustments to the UI based on patterns of misconception that the participants noted.

Storyboarding for UX

Storyboards are sequences of images with annotation describing how a process or product functions through a visual narrative.

One of the easiest ways to start a storyboard is to download a commonly available template. A search for "storyboard templates" will yield many options. These have spaces for drawing a picture and adding notes under them. Use one of these templates to draw a rough sketch of your idea. If a higher fidelity storyboard is needed you can recreate this in its final form on the computer. Revise the storyboard until it effectively tells the story you need to convey about the use of the product.

Aim for a 3 by 3 or a 4 by 4 layout per page as any more images make it difficult for the viewer to connect all the images together and see them as a whole. If the rendering of the image is not clear enough, add notes that explain the action.

To create the right mindset:
- You don't need to be an artist or make perfect pictures.
- Use whatever tools you are comfortable with.
- When presenting to others, emphasize the function of the storyboards and not the artwork.

When to use: When you need to show an experience beyond the screen designs.

Difficulty: Average   **Time:** 4 Hours   **Participants:** 1+

Storyboarding for UX Example

A complicated feature set is being proposed for an internal software product. The team wants a visual example of how the feature will be used in order to add clarity and find ways to refine the features. This method is perfect for this scenario because it makes complex topics easy to understand and brings the nuances to life in a clear way for all stakeholders.

Create a Grid System: Create a series of squares, either 3 by 3 or 4 by 4. Use multiple pages if needed.

Draw Imagery: Draw visuals that show all of the key moments that relate to the new feature set. Demonstrate how it fits into the overall flow.

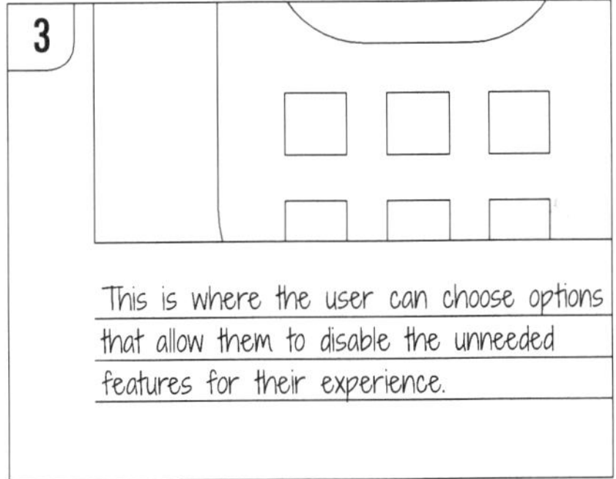

Add Notation: Below each square add written notation to support the action above it.

Review Storyboard: Now the team has a tool that gets everyone on the same page. They are able to discuss the features and find ways to further improve them.

Surveys

UX surveys are a tool for gathering information from a target audience.

Start by writing down the things you would like to discover from the participants. Begin writing questions that will provide answers to these topics. As you draft the survey it can be helpful to add a note to each question about what you are trying to learn and what you will do with the answer. Oftentimes this will help you eliminate unnecessary questions. It will also guide you to good follow-up questions. Another approach is to use the results of user interviews to inspire your questions. This lets you validate that what you found with a few interviews is true of a much larger population of people.

Once ready, prepare the survey in paper or digital form and present it to users. After enough results are gathered analyze the results to identify patterns. A digital survey tool will greatly assist in the delivery and analysis of surveys.

Properties of good survey questions:
- The question is not leading or biased.
- Everyone will interpret it in the same way.
- The answers are mutually exclusive.
- Avoid double barrel questions that ask two things at once.
- Always provide an opt-out in case the question doesn't apply.

When to use: To gather feedback and demographics and to validate findings.

Difficulty: Hard   **Time:** 2 Days   **Participants:** 100+

Surveys Example

A research team wants to understand how voters learn about candidates for upcoming elections. They have just completed a series of interviews with 8 voters. A survey will allow them to see how their discoveries apply to the larger population.

Write the Questions: The team plans the survey based on the interview results by writing out each question and the available answers.

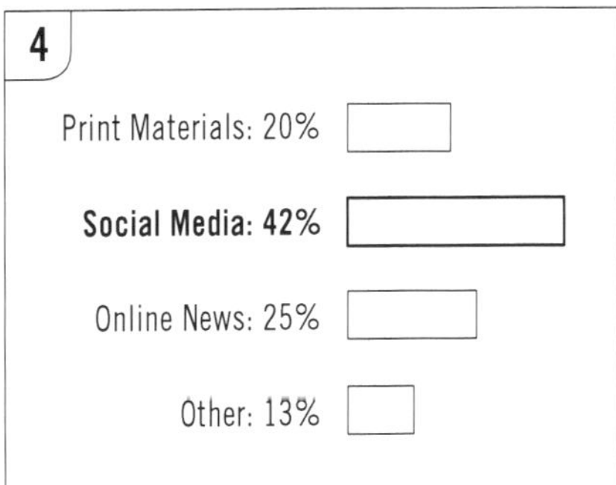

Justify Each Question: As they write each question they also write out why it should be included and what they hope to learn. This helps them trim out questions that don't add value.

Conduct the Survey: The survey is distributed to the intended audience.

Report the Results: The survey results are collected. The team writes a concise summary of the findings.

Formalize Next Steps: With solid data the team has a much better understanding of the common ways voters research candidates.

System Usability Scale

A fixed set of 10 statements to evaluate the usability of a system.

After a usability test, present users with the following questions:

1. I think that I would like to use this system frequently.

2. I found the system unnecessarily complex.

3. I thought the system was easy to use.

4. I think that I would need the support of a technical person to be able to use this system.

5. I found the various functions in this system were well integrated.

6. I thought there was too much inconsistency in this system.

7. I would imagine that most people would learn to use this system very quickly.

8. I found the system very cumbersome to use.

9. I felt very confident using the system.

10. I needed to learn a lot of things before I could get going with this system.

The answers are on a scale from 1–5. One means the participant strongly disagrees and five means they strongly agree.

- For the odd-numbered questions, subtract 1 from the response.
- For the even-numbered questions, subtract the response from 5.
- Add up all the points and multiply them by 2.5.

When to use: When you need to quantify a system's usability.

Difficulty: Average   **Time:** 1 Hour   **Participants:** 1+

System Usability Scale Example

A grocery delivery service is planning to continuously improve their customer interface over the course of many months. The team would like a metric to help them evaluate how the overall usability of the system is improving. The system usability scale is perfect because it provides a quantitative value representing the usability and can be used to compare many versions of the same system.

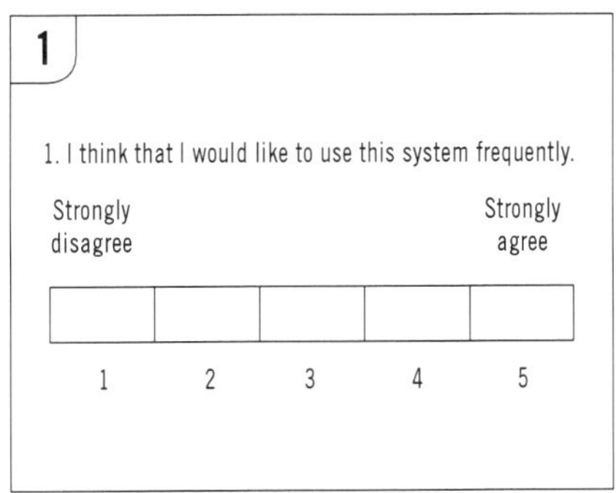

Set Up the Test: The team prepares the 10 question survey as described on page 92.

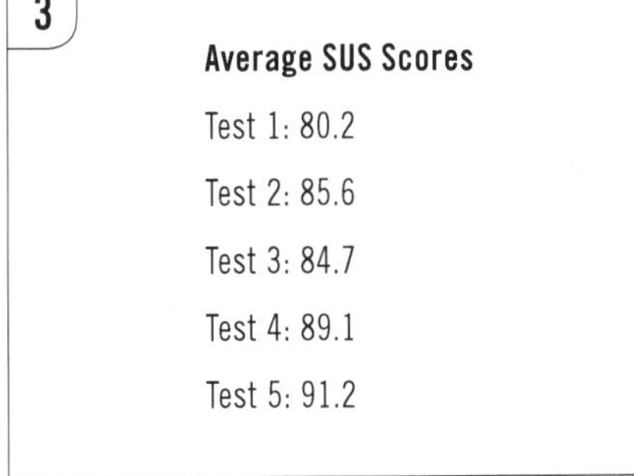

Collect Data: After each usability test of the system the participant is asked to complete the questionnaire. The resulting SUS score is then calculated.

Average SUS Scores

Test 1: 80.2

Test 2: 85.6

Test 3: 84.7

Test 4: 89.1

Test 5: 91.2

Average the Results: The results from each group of participants for a given usability test are averaged.

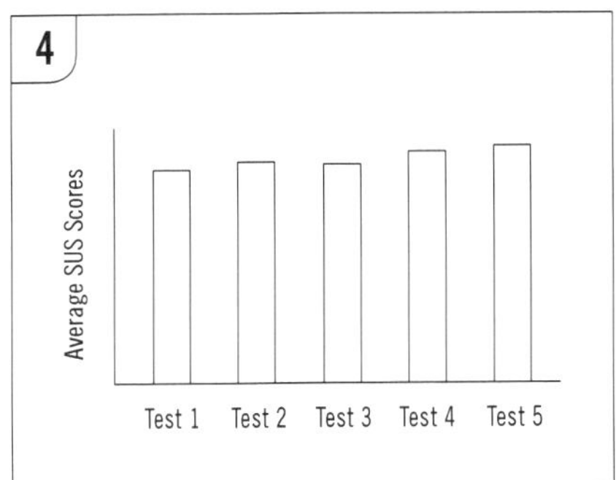

Plot the Results: A graph showing the average SUS score over time is created showing how the SUS score varies over time.

Share Metrics: Now the team has a metric to assess the improvements, and can share this to indicate progress to stakeholders.

Brooke, John. "SUS-A quick and dirty usability scale." Usability evaluation in industry 189.194 (1996): 4-7.

Teachback

Teachback is when a person interviews subject matter experts on a topic and then teaches it back to them until it's fully understood.

Start by gathering multiple experts familiar with the topic and ask them to teach it to them one at a time. After the expert explains, teach it back to the experts and they correct any misconceptions or errors. The teachback sessions should be recorded and viewed as needed. After a number of teachback sessions, you should have a better understanding of the topic or feature.

The experts could be anyone from a technical person, a manager or a front-line employee. The key is to seek understanding of the nuances surrounding a topic. This can be very helpful for situations where a designer must attempt to rapidly understand a very complex task in order to find ways to improve it.

In other situations this is referred to as "active listening." In general this is just a great habit to get into to make sure you are listening and not applying your own assumptions or biases to a situation.

When to use: When a topic or feature is very complex and difficult to quickly explain.

Difficulty: Average　　　　**Time:** 1 Hour　　　　**Participants:** 5+

Teachback Example

A complex purchase order system is being revised. The team needs to understand the workflow so they can propose improvements. The teachback method allows them to learn the process and repeat it back ensuring that they are accurately interpreting the instructions.

Gather Experts: For this scenario a data entry person, a manager and a trainer are gathered.

Start Initial Instruction: The data entry person teaches how the current process works.

Begin Teachback Session: The researcher teaches the process back to the expert. The expert should correct any mistakes.

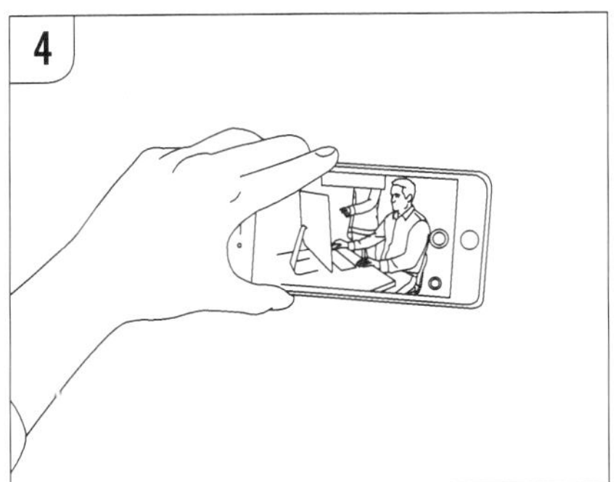

Record Session: Record each teachback session to capture the session and allow for later review.

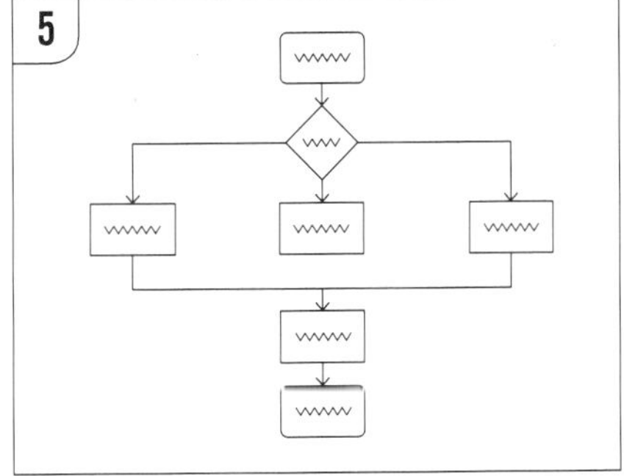

Interpret Results: Document the process in some way, and then use other UX methods to develop the digital system.

Trade-Off Sliders

Trade-off sliders visualize the importance of a list of items to help plan priorities and create focus.

Trade-off sliders are a team exercise and are not a final deliverable. Start by creating a list of key aspects of the project. Each aspect has a horizontal line with level indicators going from low to high. Stakeholders work together to discuss the value of the key components the point being that at some level one has more value than another. Markers should able to be move up and down, as the group decides where to place them for each component.

Aspects for each line can be based on any property related to the product: features, costs, size, weight, color or any other factor related to the product. Imagine for example you're designing a new mobile telephone and you have to decide what the most important properties will be. What should it cost? How large should it be? How long should the battery last? How much should it weigh? Defining these priorities can allow the team to move forward with a common vision.

When to use: To create consensus on what aspects to focus on.

Difficulty: Average   **Time:** 4 Hours   **Participants:** 2+

Trade-Off Sliders Example

In this example core features of a digital product are being considered. A team consensus needs to be determined. This method makes sense because it allows the team to visually see what others are thinking and to set priorities as a group.

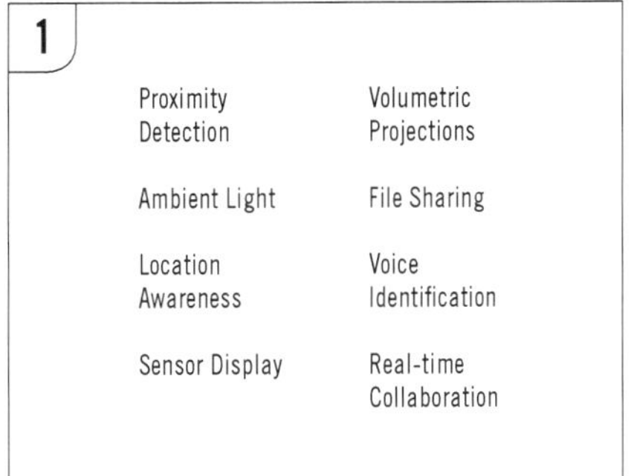

Create Key Aspects List: Create a list of words that represent the key aspects of the item being reviewed.

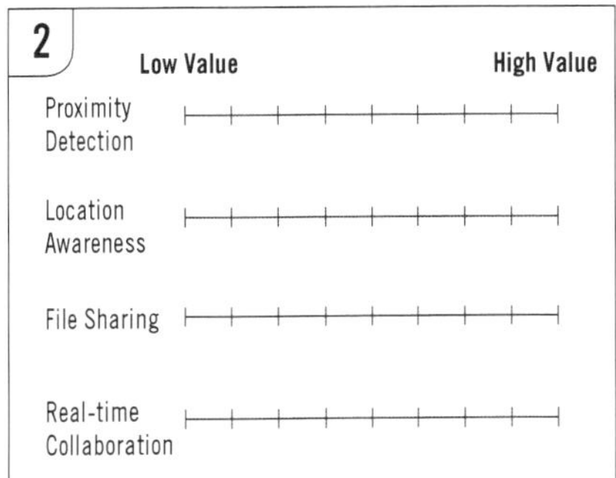

Create Indicator Scale: Create horizontal lines with evenly spaced out indicator marks to indicate the value of the feature to the users. The scale goes from low to high value.

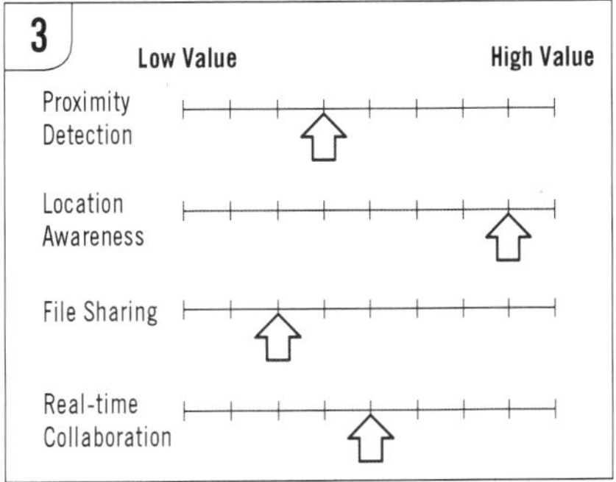

Explore: Work with stakeholders to place arrow markers that indicate the perceived value.

Discuss: Discuss thoughts on each position and adjust the markers as the team debates the aspects. This step is an important part for this method.

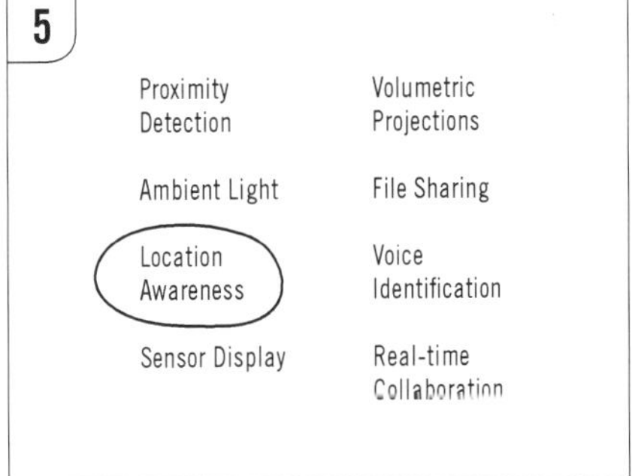

Finalize Decision: When the team agrees upon the final position of the markers, the key aspects are determined.

UX Curve

UX curve is a retrospective method that evaluates the user's experience over time through the use of a linear diagram that plots out key changes.

To set up the diagram, first create a vertical line on the left side with the top representing the positive and the bottom representing the negative moments of the experience. Then draw a horizontal line that represents time from the middle of the vertical line across to the other side. Once the user is finished with their experience (system or product), ask them to draw a curve line on the diagram from the left to the right marking peaks and lows of their experience. Ask them to note on the chart what happened at each of these high and low points, or any other notable experiences.

One variation is to create the chart on behalf of the participant as they work through the experience. After the experience is over review the diagram with the participant and discuss the high/low points you observed.

When to use: At the end of a user's experience when they are able to reflect.

Difficulty: Average   **Time:** 4 Hours   **Participants:** 2+

UX Curve Example

Major changes to an elderly health care system are being made. They want to consider the experience from start to finish. This method works well because it maps the experience over time and indicates high and low points.

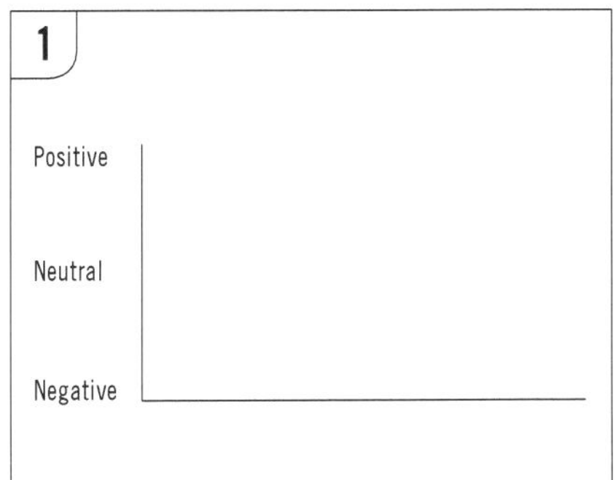

Diagram Set Up: Create a vertical axis at the left end with the top being positive and the bottom negative. Then create a horizontal axis to represent time.

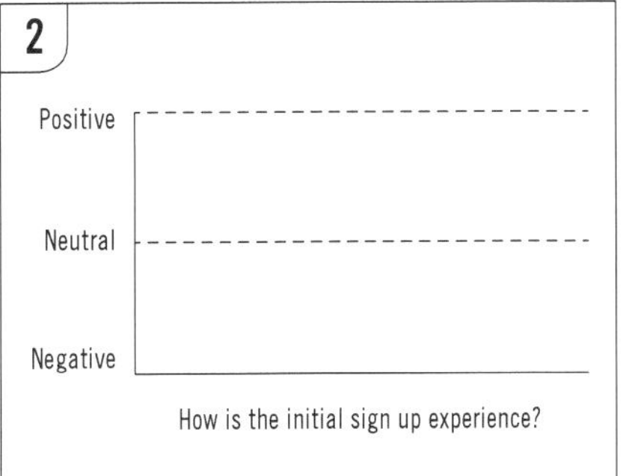

Determine Question: Write a short statement of what you want to learn at the bottom of the horizontal axis.

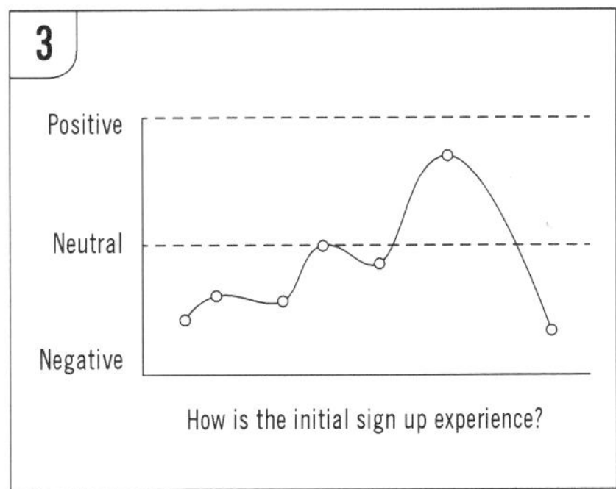

Plot Experience: Have the participants plot out their experience on the UX curve. They should add points for memorable moments in the experience.

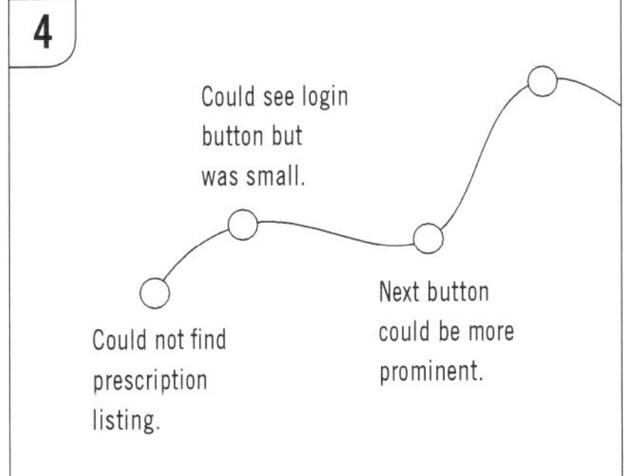

Plot Notation: Next to each plot point, have them notate what happened.

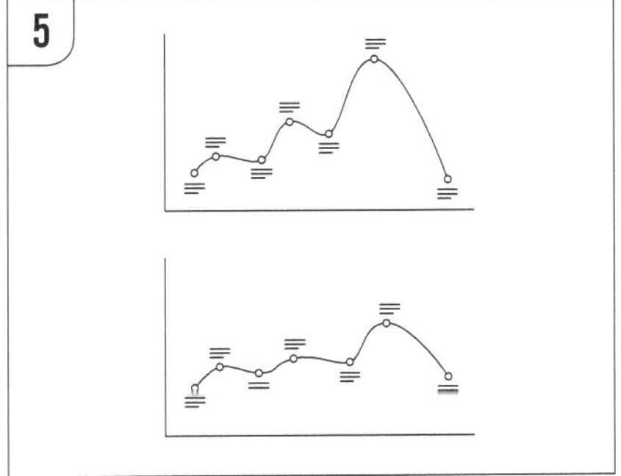

Compare Curves: When multiple UX curves are complete, compare to see patterns. Either make changes or use another UX method in that area to learn more.

Value Proposition Generation

Value proposition generation is a concise statement that quickly summarizes the vision for a product.

Begin by giving each team member a few printed copies of the value proposition template shown below. Have each person fill out 1 to 3 value propositions until they feel they have a good grasp on the approach. Write the template on a whiteboard with lots of room to fill in the blanks. Have team members add options for each blank. As a group, negotiate towards a single statement.

Value Proposition Template

For _________ (target customer) who _________ (statement of the need or opportunity) our _________ (product/service name) is _________ (product category) that _________ (statement of benefit).

The result of this is a common vision and purpose for the product. Even better, you have a succinct artifact for describing your product to anyone, such as new team members, upper management, customers or investors.

When to use: At the beginning when defining the vision or purpose of the project.

Difficulty: Easy   **Time:** 1 Hour   **Participants:** 2+

Value Proposition
Generation Example

In this example a company that sells home security devices is exploring ideas for products that will help parents monitor and protect their children. The team has many ideas and would like to form a unified vision for the product. A value proposition generation will help them by creating a concise vision statement.

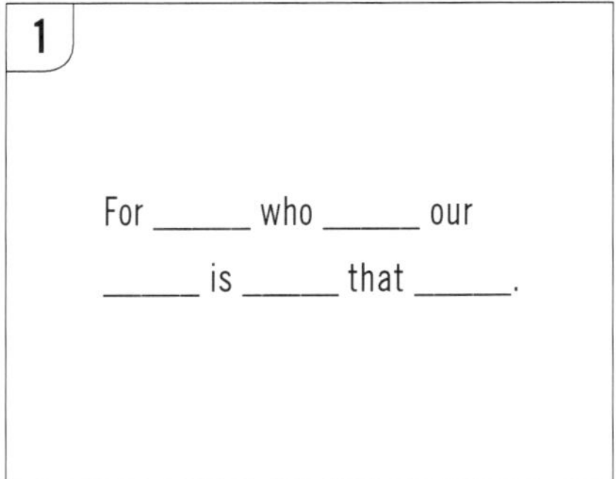

Review Template: The team assembles and reviews the value proposition template (page 100).

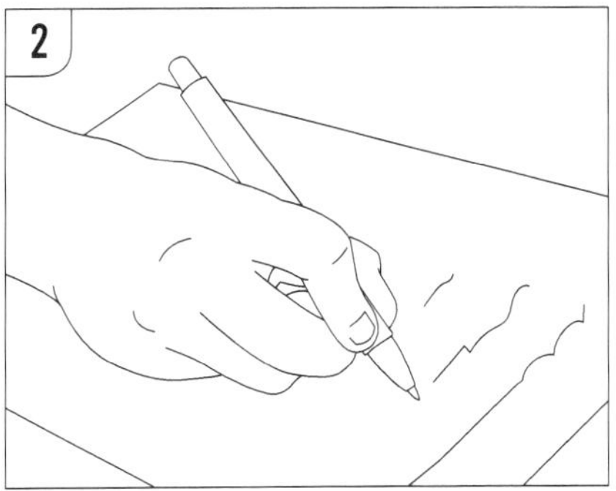

Write and Identify: Take 10 minutes to allow each member to independently write down ideas for each blank and identify their favorite idea for each space.

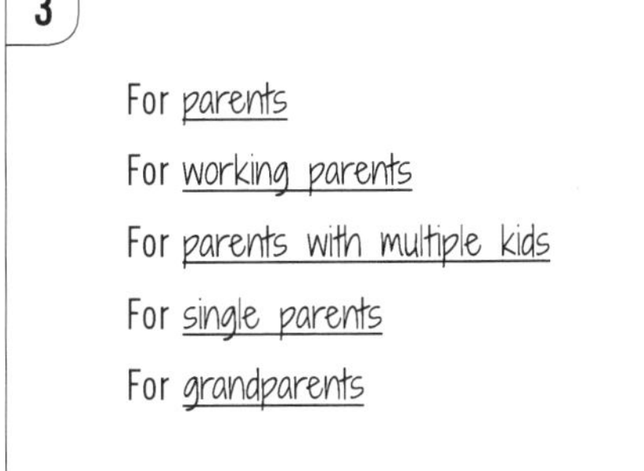

Collect the Results: For each space in the template a list is created showing everyone's favorite idea.

Reach a Consensus: The team discusses the options until they come to an agreement for each blank. The final value proposition generation statement is produced.

Method Reference: This template was originally created by Geoff Moore in his book *Crossing The Chasm*. This great book is a resource in the area of marketing and selling disruptive products.

Wizard of Oz Studies

Wizard of Oz studies are when users test theoretical systems through simulated scenarios controlled by an unseen moderator.

Start by setting up the testing area. For the moderator (i.e., Wizard), either place them behind a two-way mirror or set up a webcam so they can see from a different room. Inform the participant to enter the testing area and work through the simulated task. As the participant works through the task, the moderator will control the environment so that the interaction is as authentic as possible. The participant does not need to know the interaction is simulated or controlled by an unseen person.

An option is to either prepare a script or learn as you go by improvising the test. A script will improve the consistency but can be time consuming to create. A script does ensure you deliver the same test each time and it provides a place to document findings as you go. In contrast, improvising will help you discover less specific global issues that will help you prepare an initial script for the test.

When to use: When an iterative design needs to be tested and is too complex for a working system to be created.

Difficulty: Average   **Time:** 4 Hours   **Participants:** 2+

Wizard of Oz Studies Example

In this example a voice controlled system for delivering cooking instructions is being tested. They want to see if participants can use the system while perform cooking tasks. This method works well for this scenario since it allows the tester to simulate the voice of the system without having to build it.

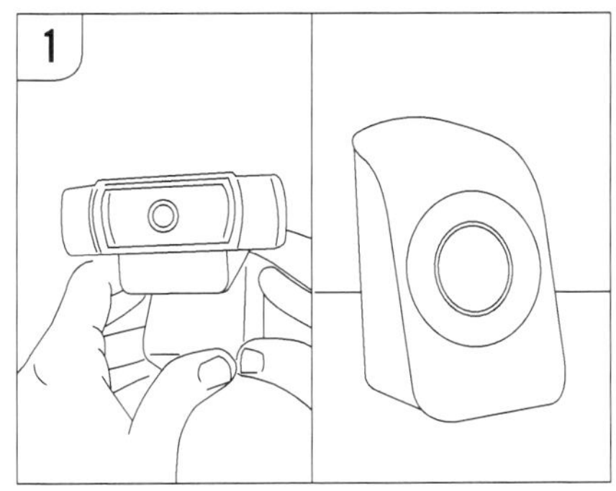

Set Up Testing Area: For this scenario a web camera and speaker are positioned in an area with cooking supplies.

Start Task: Participant enters the test area and states "ready to start" to activate the system.

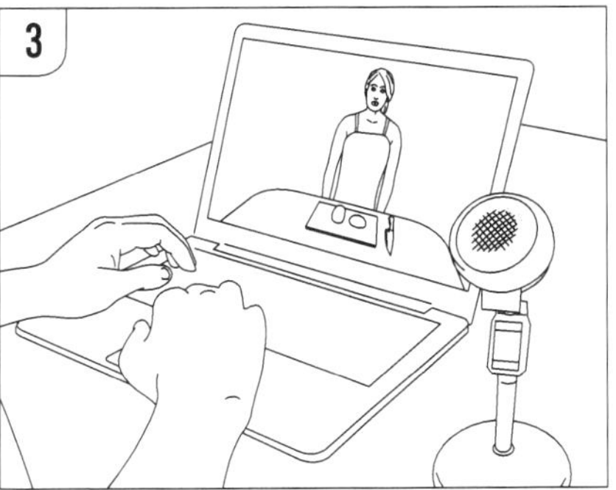

Give Instructions: From a different room (viewing from the web camera) the "wizard" gives instructions to simulate the voice response system using a prepared script.

Work through Tasks: The participant uses the simulated audio system to complete the assigned tasks.

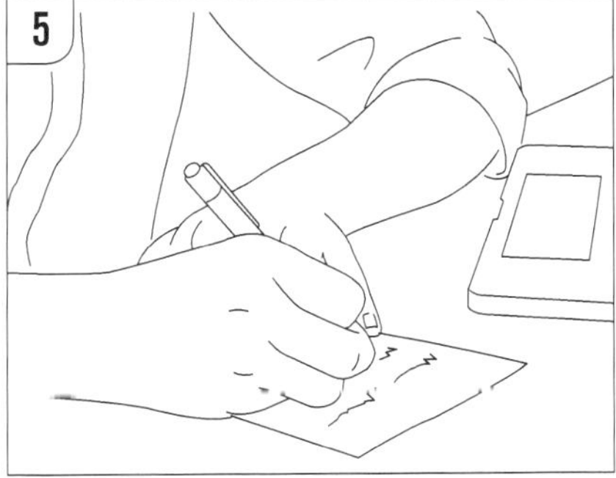

Review and Repeat: After the scenario is completed, review the results and make adjustments to the script for the next participant. Repeat the test as needed.

REFERENCES

Arvayo, Diana. 2016. UX Research with Backcasting Method. <https://dribbble.com/shots/2579573-UX-Research-with-Backcasting-Method>.

Bernard, Russell H. 1998. Handbook of Methods in Cultural Anthropology.

Bias, R.G. 1994. The Pluralistic Usability Walkthrough: Coordinated Empathies, in J. Nielsen & R. Mack - Usability Inspection Methods.

Blackmon, M. H. Polson, P.G. Muneo, K & Lewis, C. 2002. Cognitive Walkthrough for the Web CHI 2002 vol.4 No.1 pg 463–470.

Brown, Dan. 2010. Communicating Design: Developing Web Site Documentation for Design and Planning.

Budd, Andy. 2008. Guerilla Usability Testing. <https://www.slideshare.net/andybudd/guerilla-usability-testing/28-Recruiting_test_subjects_Client_contacts>.

Buley, Leah. 2013. The user experience team of one: a research and design survival guide.

Cable, Steve. 2011. Communicating the User Experience: a Practical Guide For Creating Useful UX Documentation. Wiley. http://www.books24x7.com/marc.asp?bookid=44993.

Card, Stuart K., and Moran, Thomas P., and Newell, Allen. 1980. The keystroke-level model for user performance time with interactive systems.

Carroll, J. M. and Rosson, M. B. 1992. Getting around the task-artifact cycle: How to make claims and design by scenario.

Design Kit. Photojournal. <http://www.designkit.org/methods/65>.

Doncaster, Paul. 2014. The UX Five-Second Rules: Guidelines for User Experience Design's Simplest Testing Technique.

d.school. Method: I Like, I Wish, What If. <https://dschool-old.stanford.edu/wp-content/themes/dschool/method-cards/i-like-i-wish-what-if.pdf>.

Faranello, Scott. 2016. Practical UX Design.

Farnworth, Demian. 2014. Empathy Maps: A Complete Guide to Crawling Inside Your Customer's Head. <https://www.copyblogger.com/empathy-maps/>.

The Five Whys. <http://www.designkit.org/methods/66>.

Flowerdew-Clarke, Mellissa. 2014. How to Run Successful Stakeholder, User & Content Workshops. <http://blog.building-blocks.com/insights/how-to-run-successful-client-user-content-workshops>.

Garrett, Jesse James. 2003. The elements of user experience. Indianapolis: New Riders Publ.

Goodman, Elizabeth, and Kuniavsky, Mike, and Moed, Andrea. 2012. Observing the User Experience. Second Edition: A Practitioner's Guide to User Research.

Goodwin, Kim. 2009. Designing for the Digital Age: How to Create Human-Centered Products and Services.

Gothelf, Jeff. 2013. Lean UX: Applying Lean Principles to Improve User Experience.

Harley, Aurora. 2016. Usability Testing of Icons. <https://www.nngroup.com/articles/icon-testing/>.

Hayes, Bob E. 2008. Measuring Customer Satisfaction and Loyalty, Third Edition: Survey Design, Use, and Statistical Analysis Methods.

Jungk, Robert, and Norbert Müllert. 1987. Future workshops: how to create desirable futures. London: Institute for Social Inventions.

Kalbach, James. 2016. Mapping Experiences: A Complete Guide to Creating Value through Journeys, Blueprints, and Diagrams.

Kelley, J. F. Where did the usability term Wizard of Oz come from? <http://www.musicman.net/oz.html>.

Krug, Steve. 2017. Don't make me think!: a common sense approach to Web usability. [Berkley]: New Riders.

Krug, Steve. 2009. Rocket Surgery made Easy: The Do-It-yourself Guide to Finding and Fixing Usability Problems. New Riders.

Kujala, S., Roto, V., Vaananen-Vainio-Mattila, K., Karapanos, E., Sinnela, A. 2011. UX Curve: A Method for Evaluating Long-Term User Experience. Interacting with Computers. <http://dx.doi.org/10.1016/j.intcom.2011.06.005>.

Kujala, S., Walsh, T., Nurkka, T., Crisan, M. (2013). Sentence Completion for Understanding Users and Evaluating User Experience. Interacting with Computers, 26, 3, 238-255.

León, Misael. 2015. 10 UX Techniques for Creating Products People Love. <https://nearsoft.com/blog/10-ux-techniques-for-creating-products-people-will-love/>.

Lowdermilk, Travis. 2013. User-centered design: [a developer's guide to building user-friendly applications]. Beijing: O'Reilly Media. <http://search.ebscohost.com/login.aspx?direct=true&scope=site&db=nlebk&db=nlabk&AN=561769>.

Lupton, Ellen. 2011. Graphic design thinking: beyond brainstorming. New York: Princeton Architectural Press.

McGinn, Jennifer, and Chang, Ana Ramirez. Journal of Usability Studies, Volume 8, Issue 3. RITE+Krug: A Combination of Usability Test Methods for Agile Design.

McMullin, Jess. 2010. Business Origami - paper prototyping for systems and service design <https://www.slideshare.net/jessmcmullin/business-origami-paper-prototyping-for-systems-and-service-design>.

Moore, Geoffrey A. 2006. Crossing the Chasm: Marketing and Selling High-Tech Products to Mainstream Customers.

Mulder, Steve. 2006. The User Is Always Right: A Practical Guide to Creating and Using Personas for the Web.

Nielsen, Jakob. 1995. 10 Usability Heuristics for User Interface Design. <https://www.nngroup.com/articles/ten-usability-heuristics/>.

Nielsen, Jakob, and Molich, Rolf. 1990. Heuristic evaluation of user interfaces.

Nielsen, Jakob. 2000. Why You Only Need to Test with 5 Users. <https://www.nngroup.com/articles/why-you-only-need-to-test-with-5-users/>.

Osterwalder, Alexander, and Pigneur, Yves. 2010. Business Model Generation: A Handbook for Visionaries, Game Changes, and Challengers.

Pannafino, James. 2012. Interdisciplinary Interaction Design: a visual guide to basic theories, models and ideas for thinking and designing for interactive web design and digital device experiences.

Paul, Celeste Lyn. 2008. Journal of Usability Studies, Vol. 4, Issue 1. A Modified Delphi Approach to a New Card Sorting Methodology.

Perfetti, Christine. 2007. 5-Second Tests: Measuring Your Site's Content Pages. <https://articles.uie.com/five_second_test/>.

Ratcliffe, Lindsay, and Marc McNeill. 2012. Agile experience design: a digital designer's guide to agile, lean, and continuous. Berkeley, Calif: New Riders.

Rohrer, Christian. 2014. When to Use Which User-Experience Research Methods <https://www.nngroup.com/articles/which-ux-research-methods/>.

Ross, Jim. 2013. User Research Methods: Has-beens and Stars. <https://www.uxmatters.com/mt/archives/2013/05/user-research-methods-has-beens-and-stars.php>.

Rubin, Jeffrey, and Chisnell, Dana. 2008. Handbook of Usability Testing: How to Plan, Design, and Conduct Effective Tests.

Ruf, Ann-Sofie. 2016. Method Mondays: Never Stop Learning <http://boxesandarrows.com/method-mondays-never-stop-learning/>.

Sauro, Jeff. 2010. A Practical Guide to Measuring Usability: 72 Answers to the Most Common Questions about Quantifying the Usability of Websites and Software.

Sauro, Jeff. 2011. A Practical Guide to the System Usability Scale: Background, Benchmarks & Best Practices.

Sauro, Jeff. 2011. Getting The First Click Right. <https://measuringu.com/first-click/>.

Sauro, Jeff, and Lewis, James R. 2016. Quantifying the User Experience, Second Edition: Practical Statistics for User Research.

Simon, David Peter. 2017. UX Booth. The Art of Guerrilla Usability Testing. <http://www.uxbooth.com/articles/the-art-of-guerrilla-usability-testing/>.

Sinha, Rashmi. 2003. Beyond cardsorting: Free-listing methods to explore user categorizations. <http://boxesandarrows.com/beyond-cardsorting-free-listing-methods-to-explore-user-categorizations/>.

Siroker, Dan, and Pete Koomen. 2013. A/B testing: the most powerful way to turn clicks into customers.

Spencer, Donna. D009. Card Sorting: Designing Usable Categories.

Tanner, Jacqueline. 2015. UX Research Methods. <https://blog.prototypr.io/ux-research-methods-acb80b141bdc>.

Unger, Russ, and Carolyn Chandler. 2012. A project guide to UX design: for user experience designers in the field or in the making. Berkeley, Calif: New Riders.

Usability.gov. First Click Testing. <https://www.usability.gov/how-to-and-tools/methods/first-click-testing.html>.

Usability.gov. System Usability Scale (SUS). <https://www.usability.gov/how-to-and-tools/methods/system-usability-scale.html>.

UX Booth. March 29, 2017. Complete Beginner's Guide to Analytics. <http://www.uxbooth.com/articles/complete-beginners-guide-to-web-analytics-and-measurement>.

Wikipedia. RITE Method. <https://en.wikipedia.org/wiki/RITE_Method>.

Wilson, Chauncey. 2011. UXD Method: Bodystorming. <http://dux.typepad.com/dux/2011/04/uxd-method-11-of-100-bodystorming.html>.

Wilson, Chauncey. 2011. UXD Method: Teachback. <http://dux.typepad.com/dux/2011/05/method-12-of-100teachback.html>.

IMAGE CREDITS

INTERDISCIPLINARY

INTERACTION DESIGN

A VISUAL GUIDE

TO BASIC THEORIES, MODELS
AND IDEAS FOR THINKING AND
DESIGNING FOR INTERACTIVE
WEB DESIGN AND DIGITAL
DEVICE EXPERIENCES

JAMES PANNAFINO

SECOND EDITION, REVISED AND EXPANDED

Get more information at: **www.interactiondesignbook.com**

Ask your library or bookstore to order: 978-0-9826348-2-0

Or purchase directly from www.amazon.com

A quick look at Interdisciplinary Interaction Design

Interaction design has many dimensions to it. It addresses how people deal with words, read images, explore physical space, think about time and motion, and how actions and responses affect human behavior. Various disciplines make up interaction design, such as industrial design, cognitive psychology, user interface design and many others.

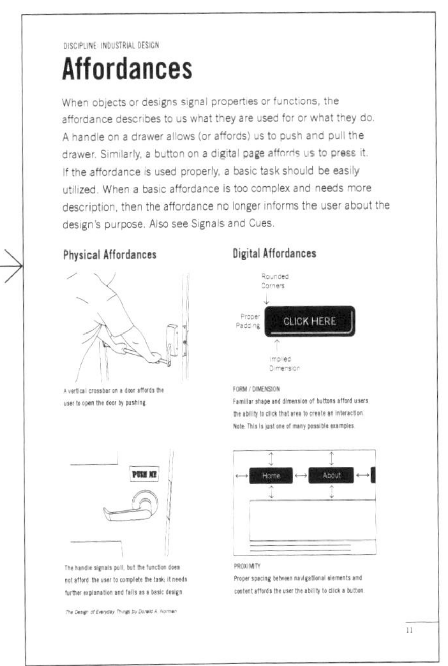

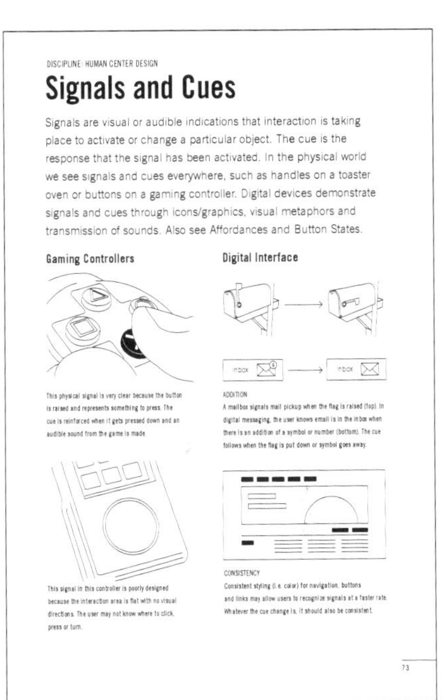

It is my hope that this book is a starting point for creating a visual language to enhance the understanding of interdisciplinary theories within interaction design. The book uses concise descriptions, visual metaphors and comparative diagrams to explain each term's meaning. Many ideas in this book are based on timeless principles that will function in varying contexts.

The Web Designer's Idea Book Volume 4

Get more information at: **www.thewebdesignersideabook.com**
Buy directly from Amazon.com today: http://a.co/iNwtxY6

Looking for inspiration for your latest web design project?
Featuring more than 650 examples of the latest trends, this
fourth volume of *The Web Designer's Idea Book* is overflowing
with visual inspiration.

Arranged categorically, this fully illustrated guide puts important
topics like design styles, elements, themes and responsive design
at your fingertips. This new volume also includes a detailed
discussion of portfolios to help you stay ahead of the pack and
keep your portfolio fresh and relevant.

The Mobile Web Designer's Idea Book

Get more information at: **www.thewebdesignersideabook.com**
Buy directly from Amazon.com today: http://a.co/18S25yu

Are you interested in trends on the mobile web? Curious to
see how designers approach responsive design for various
components of the mobile web? Want to see how tailored mobile
specific sites function compared to responsive sites? If so
The Mobile Web Designer's Idea Book does all of this and more.
Much like the other Idea Books the core focus is on collecting
samples, providing inspiration and analyzing various patterns. If
you're passionate about the mobile web, this inspiration tool will
be your best friend.